# MODERN FIGHTING AIRCRAFT
# F-16
## FIGHTING FALCON

Published by Arco Publishing, Inc

New York

# A Salamander Book

Published by Arco Publishing, Inc.,
215 Park Avenue South,
New York, New York 10003,
United States of America.

© Salamander Books Ltd., 1983.

Library of Congress Cataloging in Publication Data

Richardson, Douglas.
  F-16 Fighting Falcon

  (Modern fighting aircraft; 2)
  "A Salamander book."
  1. F-16 (Fighter planes) I. Title. II. Series.
UG1242.F5R5   1983      358.4'3      83-12239
ISBN 0-668-05903-6

All correspondence should be
addressed to Salamander Books Ltd.,
Salamander House, 27 Old Gloucester
Street, London WC1N 3AF, United
Kingdom.

# Credits

**Project Manager**: Ray Bonds

**Editor**: Bernard Fitzsimons

**Designer**: Rod Teasdale

**Diagrams**: TIGA
(© Salamander Books Ltd.)

**Three-views, cutaway drawing and
colour profiles**: © Pilot Press Ltd.

**Scrap line drawings**: Mike Badrocke
(© Salamander Books Ltd.)

**Jacket**: Kai Choi

# Contents

# Acknowledgements

This book would not have been possible
without the unstinting help over the
years of current and former members of
the public relations department at the
Fort Worth Division of General
Dynamics, and of technicians on the
assembly and flight lines. Many other
companies have provided material:
apart from those credited for supplying
photographs, these include Itek, Martin
Marietta, McDonnell Douglas, and
Oldelft. Thanks are also due to many
departments and units of the USAF, to
the air arms of Belgium, Denmark, the
Netherlands and Norway, and to their
military attaches in London, and to the
Editor and Defence Editor of *Flight
International* for research facilities.

# Author

Doug Richardson is a defence journalist
specializing in the fields of aviation,
guided missiles and electronics. Editor
of *Defence Materiel*, the journal
devoted to the British defence industry,
he trained initially as an electronics
engineer, starting his career as a
technician with an R&D team working
on avionics for the Buccaneer and the
cancelled TSR-2 project.

After an electronics R&D career
encompassing such diverse areas as
radar, electronic warfare, rocket engine
control systems, computers, automatic
test equipment and missile trials, he
switched to technical journalism as a
member of the staff of the internationally
respected aerospace journal *Flight
International*, serving as Defence Editor
before moving on to become Editor of
the international technical defence
journal *Military Technology and
Economics*.

His previous work for Salamander
includes *The Illustrated Encyclopedia
of Modern Warplanes* and contributions
to *The Balance of Military Power*, and
he has also written for such technical
and defence journals as *International
Defense Review, NATO's 15 Nations,
Defence, Technologia Militar* and
*Wehrtechnik*. In 1981 he edited
*Defense Review*, a Chinese-language
report on the British defence industry
prepared for controlled circulation in
the Chinese government, industry and
armed forces.

**Filmset** by Tradespools Ltd.

**Colour** reproduction by Rodney Howe Ltd.

**Printed** in Belgium by Henri Proost et Cie.

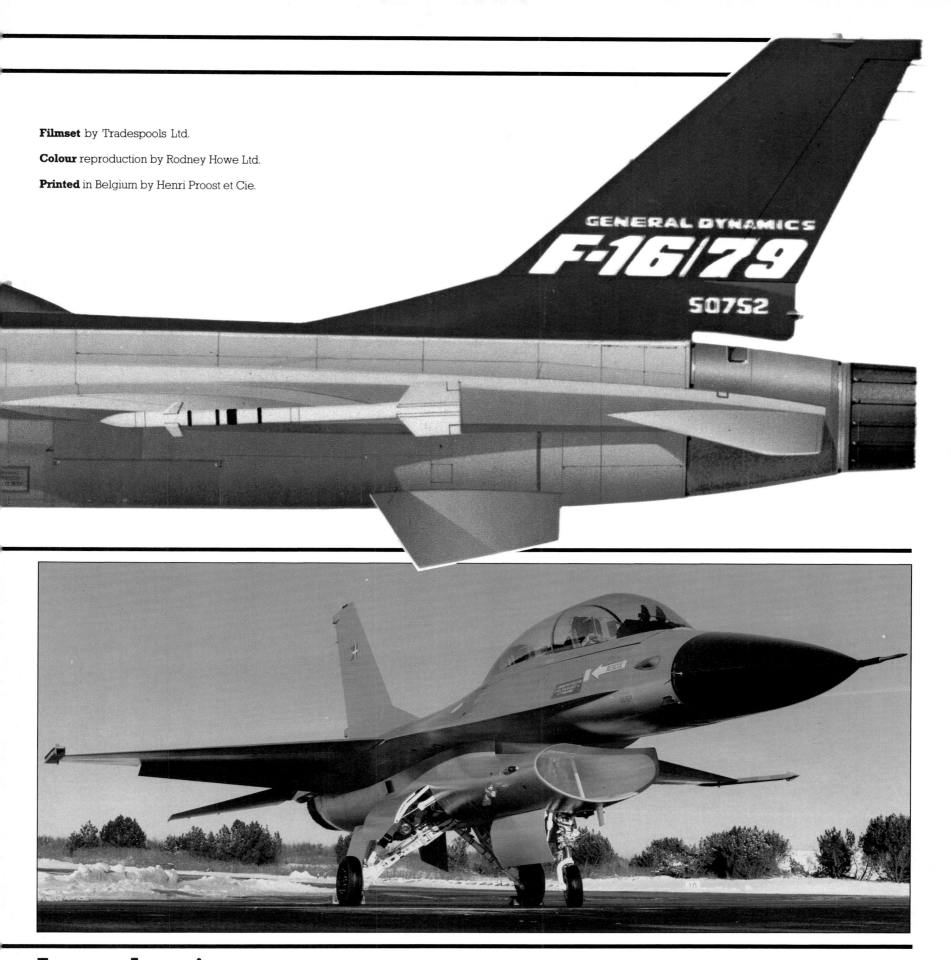

# Introduction

General Dynamics' Fighting Falcon was one of the stars of the 1977 Paris Air Show. In those not-so-distant days it was simply designated F-16 and only a handful of aircraft were flying, but the type was regarded by many observers as the hottest and probably the most controversial fighter in the Western world.

As the aircraft stood on display in the flight line, many individuals stopped to photograph it, but one in particular caught the writer's eye. Dressed in a suit of distinctly out-of-date style and equipped with a Russian camera fitted with a large telephoto lens, he was photographing the aircraft not from close up but from a range of several hundred yards.

The resulting clandestine photographs were no doubt eagerly examined in an East European Defence Ministry a few days later, but the whole exercise might have been made easier had the anonymous photographer simply marched boldly up to the F-16 and accepted one of the colour photos of the aircraft which the two GD men on duty beside it were

handing out to anyone who asked!

At a time when most of the Western European media saw the F-16 as a potential political scandal, and news reports knocking the aircraft were commonplace, the Warsaw Pact was clearly taking the new GD warplane very seriously – even if one of their intelligence-gathering methods was a trifle crude.

Subsequent events can have done little to allay their concern. Far from being the 'can of worms' which its opponents had suggested, Fighting Falcon is a highly capable aircraft likely to enter service with many more friends and allies of the West and to remain in production into the 1990s.

Moreover, the undoubted success of the initial production models seems certain to lead to future variants beyond the F-16C/D. As it enters service in ever-growing numbers, many MiG and Mirage pilots must be wondering how long they will have to wait before receiving aircraft in this performance class.

# Development

No other combat aircraft has packed as much multirole military capability into a single airframe as does the F-16 Fighting Falcon. Agile enough to outfly opponents such as third-generation MiG-21s, yet able to carry heavy ordnance loads over long ranges during strike missions, the F-16 will form a major component of Western air strength during the 1980s and 1990s. For the first time in modern fighter design 'lightweight' is not a euphemism for 'limited performance', and Fighting Falcon is a triumph for the advocates of smaller, lighter and less expensive fighters.

In following up the F-86 Sabre of the late 1940s, US fighter designers developed an expensive fascination with the sophistication made possible by improvements in technology. The larger the aircraft, the more capable it became, but while succeeding designs saw massive increases in combat capability, the price was paid in terms of both money and ever-diminishing fleet numbers. From the P-51 Mustang to the F-15 Eagle, each new US land-based fighter was on average 2·4 times more expensive than its predecessor, and Eagle production over 15 years may never reach a tenth of the 15,000 Mustangs built in a third of that time.

This philosophy was challenged briefly in the light of Korean War experience. The F-104 should have ended up a US equivalent of the MiG-21 Fishbed, but like the earlier F-100 evolved into a strike fighter instead of an air-combat fighter. Early models were used in Vietnam for a short time, but the USAF found itself having to combat the agile and lightweight MiGs of the North Vietnamese air force with the heavy and expensive F-4 Phantom – a type originally developed as an all-weather naval interceptor. The subsequent addi-tion of wing slats and a built-in 20mm cannon enhanced the aircraft's useful-ness as an air combat fighter, and the F-4E was to have a long and successful combat career, but the original design had never been intended for dogfighting.

## The Vietnam experience

Over North Vietnam, the US pilots found themselves unable to match the kill rates of the Korean War. Instead of a 10:1 or better kill ratio of the earlier conflict, they achieved at best just over 3:1, a figure which steadily fell to still lower values. For a long time, the US services claimed to have maintained permanent superiority over the MiGs, quoting rates of just over unity at worst. In practice, the ratio at times came out slightly in favour of the Vietnamese.

Part of the problem was training pro-grammes which had placed little em-phasis on air-to-air combat. The ac-cepted dogma was that the traditional dogfight had a hallowed place in the history of air fighting, but none at all in modern warfare. Even in the early 1940s, the Spitfires and Hurricanes used to defend British skies from the atten-tions of the Luftwaffe were committed to combat using elaborate pre-planned tactics which virtually denied the possi-bility of individual 'free-style' air-to-air engagements. The Luftwaffe pilots had no such illusions, and took a heavy toll of the defenders in early encounters.

With the arrival of the high-speed jet fighter, and the subsequent develop-ment of supersonic fighters, the 'no-dogfighting' dogma re-emerged virtual-ly unchanged from its early 1940s RAF form. In view of the speed of the latest warplanes, the firing time available to an attacker was thought to be so small that pilots attempting to dogfight would have little chance of hitting their targets. Long-range combat using air-to-air missiles was thought to be the likely pattern of future combat. In the skies above Korea, Suez, and the Indo-Pakis-tan border the falsehood of this theory has been demonstrated time and again. In the light of the Vietnam experience it was rejected by the USAF.

As early as 1965 the USAF began concept-formulation studies of new high-performance fighters. These in-cluded a heavy 60,000lb (27,000kg) in-terceptor/air-superiority fighter desig-nated Fighter Experimental (FX), and a lightweight Advanced Day Fighter (ADF). FX would have been heavier than the F-4 Phantom, with twin engines and a variable-geometry wing, while the 25,000lb (11,000kg) ADF design specified a thrust-to-weight ratio and wing loading intended to better the performance of the MiG-21 by a margin of 25 per cent.

The appearance of the Soviet MiG-25 Foxbat fighter in the mid-1960s created a hiatus in USAF future fighter plans. Foxbat posed the threat of the Soviet air force and its Warsaw Pact allies being equipped with Mach 3 fighters at a time when the USAF had only a handful of experimental Mach 3 YF-12 fighter pro-totypes and no plans for production of aircraft in this performance class. De-velopment of the massive North Ameri-can F-108 Rapier interceptor had begun in the late 1950s, but this Mach 3 design

**Above: Contrasting styles in fighter design – 15 years separated the first flights of the F-4 Phantom (left) and the YF-16 (right).**

**Below: Dogfighters old and new in formation provide graphic evidence that Fighting Falcon is hardly bigger than the 1940s P-51 Mustang. Note the 'bubble' canopies.**

was cancelled in September 1959, 18 months before the first of two prototypes was due to fly.

Foxbat's Mach 3 capability provoked a redirection of USAF fighter planning. The urgent goal now was to develop a design capable of matching both the existing MiG-21 and the new MiG-25, shifting the emphasis to an FX design – the F-15 – offering a high top speed and long-range missile armament.

Although on 'back-burner', the concept of a lightweight fighter similar to ADF was not dead. Two individuals who did much to keep the concept of a lightweight fighter alive were former fighter instructor Major John Boyd, and Pierre Sprey, a civilian working for the assistant Secretary of Defense for Systems Analysis.

Boyd had already had a strong influence on the FX project and was the inventor of the concept of energy manoeuvrability – a vital element in assessing fighter performance. "Let's pretend that manoeuvrability is an energy problem", he once suggested to a group of thermodynamics students. "When you manoeuvre an airplane you need energy ... you lose energy either in gaining altitude, airspeed or both.

"Normally you lose energy in turning. What happens is that your drag exceeds your thrust, and at that point you have a negative energy rate. That negative rate has to come out of altitude, airspeed or out of a combination of the two. You reach a point, even with your military afterburner, at which drag is greater than thrust. That means you have a negative vector ... you multiply net drag by velocity and that tells you how much energy you're going to have to pump up."

**Measuring performance**
At first Boyd could hardly believe that this simple idea was a new method of looking at fighter performance. Once he had accepted the fact, he considered how combinations of aerodynamics and engines could be devised to create better aircraft. "You just turn the problem of manoeuvrability around and look at it from a different viewpoint. And the result of that was obvious.... The right thrust-to-weight ratio could give you an important edge over your adversary." Fighter performance could be measured at different combinations of altitude, airspeed and manoeuvring situations in terms of what is now designated Specific Excess Power – Ps in engineering jargon.

Boyd's theory showed that the FX would require an engine with a thrust-to-weight ratio significantly better than that of current designs. The resulting F100 turbofan was not only used to power the F-15, but also created the possibility of a lightweight single-engined design of high performance.

Traditional USAF thinking prior to the

early 1970s equated light weight with short range. To some degree, this was justified in view of the technology of the time. The MiG-21 was a lightweight developed using mid-1950s technology, and the original Fishbed C day fighter gave rise to the quip among export users that it was a 'supersonic sports plane' – an aircraft with very limited range and even more limited payload.

In the late 1960s, Boyd and Sprey devised a 25,000lb (11,340kg) design designated F-XX – a dedicated air superiority fighter of high endurance. Later studies took this weight down even lower to around 17,000lb (7,700kg). The concept met much opposition, since some saw it as a threat both to traditional thinking on the subject of fighters and to the existing F-15 project.

By 1971, Boyd was working for the Air Force Prototype Study Group. Consequently, he was able to push the concept at a time when the idea of competitive flight-testing of prototype designs was returning to vogue after the massive and highly controversial Total Procurement Package contracts of the 1960s which had resulted in the F-111 and C-5 Galaxy.

Main driving force in getting the LWF project off the drawing board and into the experimental shop was Deputy Defense Secretary David A. Packard, who saw the concept of competitive prototyping as a method of reversing the ever-growing cost of new weapon systems. A series of ground rules for such prototyping exercises drawn up by Air Force Secretary Robert C. Seamans specified that funding would be limited, with initial performance goals and military specifications kept to a minimum. Contestants should not be constrained by

**Above: The Convair F-106 was built only in small numbers, but the YF-16 from the same Fort Worth plant was the first of at least 2,000.**

the existing force structure of the USAF, but should not assume that any long-term production commitment existed.

Two USAF requirements were chosen for prototyping: a medium STOL transport intended to replace the C-130 Hercules, and the lightweight fighter. These resulted in the Boeing YC-14 and McDonnell Douglas YC-15 jet transports and the YF-16 and YF-17 fighter prototypes. Instead of the 'XC-' and 'XF-' designations which would have been traditional for such programmes, the 'Y' (development) prefix was used in order to stress that a mixture of off-the-shelf and experimental technologies were being used.

The first YF-16, serial 72-1567 was rolled out at Fort Worth in December 1973, only 21 months after contract award. Following an 'unofficial' and unplanned first flight on January 20, 1974, it was used to clear the flight envelope, achieving supersonic speed on its third official sortie. Along with the second prototype it took part in the fly-off against the Northrop YF-17, and was flown against MiG-17 and MiG-21 fighters.

**Above: The YF-16s did much experimental work with ordnance and missiles. Here the second aircraft carries Paveway laser-guided bombs on underwing pylons and an Atlis laser designator under the intake.**

**Above right: Definitive F-16 configuration with the enlarged tail.**

**Above: When first rolled out the second YF-16 was painted in a blue-on-white camouflage scheme devised**

**by GD. It was later repainted in red, white and blue to match the first aircraft, then in all grey.**

Four contracts worth a total of around $100 million were placed early in 1972 under the LWF programme. General Dynamics was given $38 million to develop and fly two YF-16s, while Northrop was awarded $39 million for two prototypes of the rival YF-17. Contracts were also given to Pratt & Whitney for development of a version of the F100 turbofan specifically for single-engined installations, and to General Electric for the new and smaller YF101 engine.

In submitting a Request for Proposals (RFP) for what was now designated the Lightweight Fighter (LWF) to industry in early 1972, the USAF specified three main objectives. The resulting design should fully explore the advantages of emerging technologies, reduce the risk and uncertainties involved in full-scale development and production of a new fighter, and provide the Department of Defense with a variety of technological options available to meet military hardware needs.

Instead of trying to match the 'brochure' capability of Soviet fighters, the USAF decided to optimize the LWF for the likely conditions of future air combat – altitudes of 30,000 to 40,000ft (9,000 to 12,000m) and speeds of Mach 0.6 to 1.6 – with no attempt to equal the performance of the MiG-25 Foxbat. It was designed not for the top right-hand corner of the performance envelope, but for a wide range of flight conditions, and with the emphasis on turn rate, acceleration and range. This combination of parame-

ters would allow the resulting aircraft to intercept and engage not only existing Warsaw Pact types such as the MiG-21, MiG-23 and Su-7, but also more advanced aircraft such as developed MiG-23 versions and the Su-24 Fencer.

The choice of likely operating height would raise a few eyebrows today, when most combat aircraft must fly at treetop height in order to survive, but reflects a time before the surface-to-air missile threat had literally brought the USAF down to earth. Even in the mid-1970s, the concept of flying into hostile airspace at medium altitude under the cover of advanced ECM had still not been abandoned.

**Prototype technology**
Following industrial submissions by five companies, General Dynamics and Northrop were chosen to develop flight-test hardware, and a contract was awarded to General Dynamics on April 13, 1972. This was a 'cost plus fixed fee' contract worth $37.9 million, and covered the design, construction and test of two prototypes under the USAF designation YF-16, plus one year of flight testing.

Although development and testing of these light fighters was a technology-demonstration programme, the USAF retained the option of carrying on to develop the design into a service aircraft. The contract with GD specified an average flyaway unit cost target of $3.0 million in 1972 dollars, (rather more in

1983 prices), assuming a production run of 300 examples at a rate of 100 per year. Complete design responsibility for the aircraft lay with the contractors, in order to reduce paperwork and maintain the pace of the programme, under the direction of the Aeronautical Systems Division at Wright-Patterson AFB, which monitored both projects throughout subsequent development.

No attempt was made in designing the YF-16 to push individual technological advances: the intention was to produce and test an aircraft capable of being developed into an operational type. New technology was used in in-

**Above: According to some critics, the F-16 should have retained the YF-16 configuration shown here – a simple day fighter armed with two AIM-9, a cannon and minimal avionics.**

stances where it would have the greatest effect in meeting performance targets, but proven systems and components were retained in areas where such new technology was not required. Components and detail assemblies were designed for ease of manufacture, using low-cost materials wherever possible. Hardware was standardized wherever possible, the design of the air-

**Below: In creating the full-scale development F-16s GD engineers increased the areas of the wing, horizontal stabilizers and ventral strakes and re-configured the forward fuselage to accommodate a nose radar. The third FSD aircraft, 75-**

**0747, flew for the first time on May 3, 1977, and was the first to be fitted with the full avionics and fire-control system. This aircraft was the only F-16 to carry the two-tone dark grey-on-grey camouflage scheme.**

**Left: After completion at Fort Worth the first prototype was flown to Edwards Air Force Base aboard a Lockheed C-5A Galaxy transport. It was then re-assembled to allow flight trials to begin. First tests were high-speed taxi runs.**

frame often incorporating multi-use parts and assemblies.

Flying advanced technology features on the YF-16 gave the USAF confidence to adopt them in a service aircraft. "If we hadn't put them in the prototype, we'd still be arguing about putting them into a production airplane", F-16 director of engineering Willian C. Dietz told the US magazine *Aviation Week & Space Technology* in 1977. Although high-technology features such as relaxed stability, fly-by-wire control, wing/body blending and strakes, variable camber and the reclining seat were used to improve F-16 performance, these were not seen as high risks in terms of production or maintenance.

Specific cost goals were set at an early stage, and careful studies were carried out to establish areas where a trade-off between cost and performance or operational capability would be acceptable.

**Prototype design**

Design objective of the YF-16 was to create the maximum agility and manoeuvrability in a small aircraft with minimum avionics capable of conducting air combat operations some 500nm (575 miles/926km) from its own base.

Small size not only dictated design simplicity, but brought a series of other advantages. Factors such as material, detail design and construction being equal, airframe cost is largely dependent on airframe weight, so the move towards a smaller aircraft promised lower costs. At the same time, drag was minimized, allowing a lower thrust setting to be used during aircraft cruise, and increasing the thrust-to-weight ratio possible with any given powerplant. And as experience in Vietnam had shown, the small size of the MiG-17 and MiG-21 made them difficult to detect visually, adding to the problems of aircrew engaging these types in air combat.

One factor which helped focus USAF attention on the virtues of the YF-16 and YF-17 was the Middle East War of 1973. The USAF has always fought its wars under conditions of numerical superiority, but October of that year saw a close ally struggling to win air and battlefield superiority against forces abundantly

equipped along Soviet lines. The need of quantity as well as quality was brought home in a conflict in which one observer estimates that some 40 per cent of the Israeli fighter force was lost, or damaged to the point where it was not available for combat, within the first two days.

One influence on the size of the design was the likely avionics payload. While the LWF requirement specified minimal avionics, the design team recognized that an operational aircraft would probably require a heavier and bulkier payload of electronics. Accordingly, the decision was made not to size the basic aircraft to handle radar-guided missiles such as the AIM-7 Sparrow, but to assume an air-to-air armament of heat-seeking AIM-9 Sidewinder missiles plus a General Electric M61 cannon, while making provisions within

the design to allow Sparrow-class missiles to be incorporated at a later date, should this be desired.

Military requirements specified a load factor of 7.33g while carrying 80 per cent internal fuel. GD decided to increase this figure to 9.0g at full internal fuel, and to increase the service life of the airframe from the normal 4,000 hours to 8,000 hours.

Accepting the fact that fighters invariably end up carrying external fuel tanks, the GD team decided to capitalize on this trend. Assuming that a YF-16 pilot would use externally-carried fuel on the outbound trip to the combat zone, then fight and return on internal fuel, the design team allocated internal fuel volume accordingly, reducing the airframe size. This move shaved 1,470lb (667kg) off the airframe empty weight, and reduced all-up weight by

**Above: This head-on view of a YF-16 shows the wing leading-edge strakes and the way the wing is blended smoothly into the fuselage.**

3,300lb (1497kg). More importantly, turn rate could as a result be increased by five per cent, and acceleration by 30 per cent.

Before deciding on a configuration for the new aircraft, GD engineers considered the effect of 78 variables, running theoretical analyses and wind-tunnel tests. The latter testing totalled 1,272 hours, and was carried out at speeds from Mach 0.2 up to Mach 2.2, at angles of attack of up to 28deg and at yaw angles of up to 12deg. Parameters identified as having a significant influence on performance included wing sweep, camber and aerofoil section, inlet position and shape, the incorpora-

**Above: Rival of the YF-16 during the USAF competitive fly-off was the Northrop YF-17. Developed from the California team's P-530 Cobra, this design featured twin vertical tail fins and was powered by two General Electric YF101 'leaky turbojet' engines.**

tion of wing/fuselage blending, forebody strakes and canards, plus the number, planform and location of the tail surfaces.

Combat priorities laid down by the LWF requirements were turning performance at Mach 1·2 (demanding low wave drag), turning performance at Mach 0·9 (demanding optimum drag-at-lift), acceleration (requiring minimal wave drag) and maximum lift at Mach 0·8/40,000ft (12,000m) (again requiring optimum drag-at-lift). These conflicting

**Below: In creating the production configuration (right), GD engineers slightly increased the dimensions of the original YF-16 (left), and reprofiled the nose section to accommodate the APG-66 radar. This photograph shows the second YF-16 and the first FSD aircraft.**

demands made the selection of a wing planform difficult. In many ways, a straight wing fitted with leading edge flaps offered the best compromise, but wave drag was high. Wave drag of a swept wing would have been better, but penalties would have been paid in terms of handling qualities and drag-at-lift.

Previous fighters from the same design stable were the delta-winged F-102 Delta Dagger and F-106 Delta Dart, and the variable-geometry F-111, but neither of these proven technologies seemed right for the new fighter. Delta wings offer high volumetric efficiency, along with low structural weight and wave drag, but suffer penalties in trim drag and drag-at-lift. Variable geometry can give optimum aerodynamic performance in all flight conditions, but imposes problems at weight and balance.

The design finally adopted traded wing loading against aspect ratio to achieve the optimum balance between the conflicting demands imposed by the turn rate and acceleration requirements. Leading-edge sweep angles of 35deg, 40deg and 45deg were tested, along with six aerofoil sections. The

latter included constant thickness and camber, and designs in which these parameters were varied from root to tip. The selected design has a leading edge sweep of 40deg, an aspect ratio of 3·0 and a wing loading of 60lb/sq ft (2·53kg/sq m).

A wing of fixed camber could not have satisfied the conflicting demands of takeoff and landing, subsonic cruise, combat manoeuvring at high G levels and supersonic flight, but the use of variable camber played a major part in maintaining aircraft handling qualities and performance, particularly throughout the likely range of air combat speeds (Mach 0·8 to 1·6). It also allowed the use of a low aspect ratio and a thickness of only four per cent, factors which helped to optimize drag-at-lift and thus transonic manoeuvring.

To achieve this, the YF-16 wing was fitted with leading and trailing-edge flaps: if used throughout the flight envelope, these would help match the wing to changing Mach number and angle of attack. And instead of the slotted pattern of leading-edge flaps often used in other aircraft during takeoff and landing, the YF-16 wing incorporated a plain single-in-chord flap. Flap positions are automatically adjusted by the flight-control system.

### Design similarities
At first sight, the competing GD and Northrop designs looked very different, but both made use of moderately swept wings and long root extensions. This was no coincidence, both teams having concluded that the vortexes cast by such extensions at high angles of attack would maintain a good airflow across the wing, even beyond stalling point, thus promising good handling at high angles of attack.

Another area of advanced technology in the YF-16 design was the adoption of wing-body blending. Near the root, the wing's depth is increased to the point where it blends smoothly into the fuselage. Company engineers had originally devised this technique in the late 1940s during studies of jet-powered seaplane fighters, though the definitive Convair YF2Y fighter which flew in 1953 did not in practice use wing-body blending.

**Above: Formation take-off by the first and second full-scale development aircraft. The latter sports its third paint scheme – the all-grey finish which replaced the earlier blue-on-white and red/white/blue markings. Both aircraft are fitted with instrumented nose probes.**

The technique was also used on the Douglas Skyray and Saab 35 Draken, in both cases providing sufficient internal volume for a substantial payload of fuel.

The YF-16 centre of gravity was located far enough aft to reduce longitudinal stability and increase manoeuvrability. Since lift acted ahead of the c.g., the tailplane was required to push the tail of the aircraft up rather than down in order to maintain level flight. It thus added to the lift rather than subtracting from it as on normal designs. At supersonic speeds, the centre of pressure moved aft, reducing the amount of downward force which the horizontal tail surfaces had to apply.

To 'tame' the resulting flying characteristics, the GD design team had to provide a full-time fly-by-wire stability augmentation and flight-control system to translate the pilot's control demands into movements of the aircraft control surfaces. Without the confidence gained with the YF-16, the Air Force probably would not have adopted a fly-by-wire control system in the production aircraft, a service project director stated in 1977.

In selecting an engine for the new fighter, the GD designers had to consider not only the virtues of single and twin-engined installations, but also the effects of different engine cycles (bypass ratio and pressure ratio). The most obvious candidates were a single Pratt & Whitney F100 or a pair of General Electric YF101s. The former was already under development for use in the F-15 Eagle, and its medium bypass-ratio turbofan design offered high thrust and good fuel economy.

The Fort Worth team did look into the possibility of creating a much lighter aircraft powered by a single YF101, but studies suggested that this would be unable to meet the performance requirements. This approach was in fact to

**Right: Experimental 'lizard' camouflage scheme of dark grey, olive drab and dark green worn by two 388th TFW/16th TFTS F-16s, this one a two-seat F-16B, in 1979–80.**

be adopted in the late 1970s by Northrop, when the latter company set out to create what eventually became the F-20 Tigershark, but this is a 'shorter-legged' design less able to carry out long-range bombing missions.

The safety factors involved in single and twin-engine designs are more difficult to quantify. Discussing this problem in a technical paper on YF-16 development, Deputy Program Director Harry Hillaker stated "Many evaluations of accumulated accident-rate data have been made with varying conclusions. The number of variables involved in these evaluations make it impossible to arrive at a specific conclusion. I will debate, however, the argument that safety is the primary consideration in determining the desired number of engines." The merits of single versus twin-engined designs are still a subject of debate, and one which was later to play a significant role in persuading some nations to adopt the twin-engined F-18 Hornet rather than the GD fighter.

**First flights**

The first YF-16 prototype was rolled out at Forth Worth on December 13, 1973, a mere 21 months after GD received the $37·9 million contract. First flight of the YF-16 took place on January 20, 1974 at Edwards AFB – ahead of schedule and much to the surprise of GD pilot Phil Oestricher and all the technicians watching what should have been a high-speed taxi trial to check pitch and roll response.

As the aircraft gained speed and was rotated into a nose-up attitude, a diverging rolling oscillation built up. Distracted by this, and still relatively unfamiliar with the YF-16's high thrust-to-weight ratio, Oestricher allowed the speed to build up to around 150kt. Realizing that the horizontal tailplane had hit the runway, Oestricher decided that the best way of handling the problem was to get airborne. A brief six-minute circuit followed, and the YF-16 was successfully brought in to a smooth landing.

The subsequent investigation showed that the oscillation experienced during the roll down the runway had been pilot-induced, largely as a result of the gain of the flight-control system. The 'fix' was simple – the gain was reduced by 50 per cent while the aircraft was on the ground, then automatically raised to its full value once airborne.

**Above: The moment of liftoff as the third FSD aircraft leaves the Forth Worth runway to begin an avionics test mission. The nose radome carries the normal pattern of probe, while the small black 'teardrop' fairing immediately behind the radome is for a radar-warning receiver.**

The official first flight followed on February 2, with Oestricher once again at the controls. The prototype was taken up to 15,000ft (4,500m) with the undercarriage extended. The gear was then retracted, the speed increased to 300–350kt and 2–3g turns carried out. The sortie lasted for 90 minutes. Three days later, Oestricher took the aircraft supersonic for the first time, reaching a top speed of Mach 1·2 and remaining supersonic for five minutes. Manoeuvres at up to 5g were also carried out during this third flight of the YF-16.

By the time that the second prototype joined the programme in May of that year, temporary flying restrictions had been placed on the type following two incidents in which the F100 turbofan had lost power. Both were traced to contamination of the fuel-control valve which had caused this component to

**Above: Near-plan view of the third FSD aircraft during a sortie from Edwards Air Force Base. The muzzle port for the 20mm M61 cannon is a prominent feature on the port-side strake. The black-and-white film used has increased the contrast of non-standard markings.**

jam at the idle position, but until the problem was cleared up the YF-16 had to remain within 'dead-stick' landing distance of the runway.

To allow spinning and spin-recovery characteristics to be safely explored, along with handling at high angles of attack, a 0·3-scale flying model was flown at Edwards AFB in 1975. Built from glass fibre with an aluminium sub-structure, this was 14ft (4·27m) long, had an 8ft 9in (2·67m) wingspan and was stressed to handle loads of up to 5·5g.

**Below: Delivered in November 1977, FSD aircraft No 5 was initially used to explore aircraft handling qualities. It was later assigned to Eglin Air Force Base in Florida to take part in Seek Eagle – a USAF programme to determine the limits of the F-16's weapons carrying capability.**

### An operational fighter

Even before the second prototype had flown, the LWF programme was no longer just a technology demonstration. In April 1974 US Defense Secretary James R. Schlesinger decided that the successful LWF contender was to be developed into an operational type designated ACF (Air Combat Fighter). As flight testing of the YF-16 and the rival YF-17 continued throughout 1974, pilots from the USAF, US Navy and US government were able to evaluate both types. Trials included air-to-air combat against the A-37B Dragonfly, F-106 Delta Dart, F-4 Phantom and MiG-21. These tests were completed by the end of 1974.

Selection of the YF-16 was announced on January 13, 1975. Secretary of the Air Force John McLucas stated that performance of the GD aircraft had been 'significantly better' during the fly-off, particularly at supersonic and near-supersonic speeds. The YF-16 had also exhibited better acceleration, endurance and turning capability.

An initial development contract awarded by the USAF covered 15 development aircraft – 11 single-seat fighters and four two-seat trainers – and was worth $417·9 million. A separate $55·5 million contract to Pratt & Whitney covered engine development.

The production aircraft was effectively a slightly scaled-up version of the prototype design. The latter had not been fitted with nose radars, and original USAF planning had assumed that the ACF design would carry a small search radar similar in peformance to the Emerson APQ-159 fitted to the Northrop F-5E. The subsequent decision to adopt a more powerful multi-mode set required an increase in nose volume, nose length being extended by 7in (17·8cm), while nose diameter was increased by 4in (10·2cm). The number of access doors on the airframe was increased in the revised design, while the number of weapon stations was increased from seven to nine.

Selection of the YF-16 ended any chance that four NATO countries – Belgium, Denmark, the Netherlands and Norway, all of which were looking to replace their F-104 Starfighters – might adopt the YF-17, although Northrop pointed out that their design had been flown with prototype engines which had clocked up less than 1,000 hours of test running. Production engines would have provided eight per cent more

thrust, raising aircraft performance.

The USAF concluded that the GD aircraft outperformed the Northrop design in several areas, although the latter was superior in some respects. Around Mach 0·7, the YF-17 could outturn the YF-16, but from Mach 0·8 upwards the YF-16 was better. The GD aircraft had greater range, and was considered to be closer in standard to a production design in terms of weight, fuel capacity, and thrust-to-weight ratio.

USAF studies suggested that flyaway costs of the F-16 would be some six to seven per cent lower than those of the F-17, and that savings could also be anticipated in development and operation. Engine choice was not a factor in the selection, but the twin-engined design would have consumed 20 per cent more fuel, an important factor as the price of oil continued to rise following the 1973 Middle East War.

### US Navy interest

In the meantime, the GD aircraft remained a contender for the US Navy's contemporary NACF (Navy Air Combat Fighter) programme to replace the F-4 Phantom and A-7 Corsair. One configuration proposed by the Fort Worth team was a single-seat design using the fuselage of the two-seat trainer in order to obtain more internal volume for avionics or fuel. The YF-16 had 18cu ft (0·51cu m) of volume for internal avionics, a figure which was reduced in practice to 12·8cu ft (0·36cu m) by the installation of flight test avionics. The new proposal

**Above: An international quartet poses on a snow-cleared taxiway – production F-16s in the markings of Norway (bottom left), Netherlands (upper left), Belgium (upper right) and Denmark (bottom right). All are two-seat F-16B versions.**

would have provided up to 25cu ft (0·71cu m) of space.

The four NATO nations sent a delegation to the US in May 1974 to discuss possible LWF procurement. At that time the USAF were thinking of ordering 650 fighters, with the US Navy taking a further 800 examples. Selection of the USAF's new fighter was not scheduled until May 1975, but the European air arms wanted a decision by the end of September 1974.

This date was impossible to attain, but the deadline for USAF source selection was brought forward to January 1975 by speeding up the flight test programme. Flight refuelling was used to extend the duration of individual flight-test sorties, while the programme was revamped to avoid unnecessary duplication of flight test conditions. Instead of the two and half years normally required to complete Category 3 flight testing on a new aircraft, the YF-16 and -17 tests were completed in sufficient detail to allow source selection in January 1975, barely a year after first flight. At this point the US Navy, considering that it did not have sufficient data to make a choice, quit the LWF programme to continue its own studies of both aircraft.

Meanwhile the deadline for submission of proposals to the NATO Governments had been extended to January 1975 at the request of the US. The formal F-16 proposal was submitted on January 14, a day after the Swedish proposal (for the SAAB-Scania 37E Viggen) and a day ahead of the French (for the M53 turbofan-powered Dassault-Breguet Mirage F.1E).

The formal decision to adopt the F-16 came as no surprise when announced on June 7, 1975, although many observers noted that Belgium planned to deploy 102 aircraft rather than the anticipated 116. The resulting cost savings were intended to be invested in research and development work directed towards a new West European combat aircraft.

### F-16 production

In developing the F-16 from the YF-16, changes were kept to a minimum. Fuselage length was extended by 10in (25·4cm), while the wing area was increased by 20sq ft (1·85sq m), and fitted with two additional hard points. The horizontal tailplane was increased in size, and a jet starter was added to the F100 turbofan.

Assembly of the first full-scale production F-16 began in December 1975, and involved GD in a major modernization of its Fort Worth plant. Since the F-111 programme, the latter (officially USAF Plant 4) had been under-utilized, and had seen no major investment or updating since the 1960s. GD initially hoped to get Department of Defense funding for the modernization needed for the F-16 programme, but the US Government had already decided that it was no longer prepared to finance capital facilities needed for military projects. The Pentagon agreed that the plant would require updating, but expected GD to finance this themselves. By the summer of 1982 the company had invested $70 million, and was planning to spend $25 million more.

In laying out the production line, GD allowed for production of up to 45 aircraft per month. By the end of 1980, production was running at 16 per month and the manufacturer estimated that the current tooling could be used to build another 23–25 per month if required.

Under the 1975 agreement, a total of 348 F-16s for the European partners were to be assembled in Europe, 184 at the Fokker plant at Schiphol in the Netherlands, and 164 by SABCA at Gosselies in Belgium. The four nations are also entitled to offsets of 10 per cent of the dollar value of each aircraft sold to the USAF, and 15 per cent on aircraft sold to other export customers.

The Memorandum of Understanding covering European purchase and co-production of the F-16 ensured that the European companies involved in the project would receive work not only on USAF aircraft but also on Fighting Falcons built for Third World operators. It also stipulated the payment to the US government of a $471,000 research and development levy on the price of each aircraft delivered to the four air arms. The latter figure includes a recoupment charge for F100 R & D.

Preliminary contracts for the F-16 were placed in 1975 with European industry. It is impractical to detail all the suppliers in a programme of this mag-

**Left: Demonstration flight by two brand new F-16As of the USAF. In the clean configuration shown here the aircraft could easily outfly the MiG-21 and could probably cope with the new MiG-29 Fulcrum. These particular Fighting Falcons were delivered in April 1980.**

**Above: F-16s on the final assembly line at Fokker's Schipol plant in the Netherlands. Co-ordination and control of the multi-national assembly programme was a formidable management task comparable to that of the Apollo space programme.**

nitude, but the main contracts were awarded as follows.

Two aircraft assembly lines were set up, one at the SABCA plant at Gosselies in Belgium, where Belgian and Danish airframes are assembled, the other at the Fokker plant at Schiphol-Oost in the Netherlands. At the same time, the Belgian company SONACA – formerly Fairey SA – was reconstituted with new management and was contracted to build the aft fuselage.

Assembly of aircraft for the Netherlands and Norway is handled by Fokker, who also build the centre fuselage, the leading edge flaps, the trailing edge panel and flaperon. SABCA facilities at Gosselies and Haren in Belgium tackle the wing structure box and assembly of the complete wing. Other components such as the vertical fin box and the wing and centreline pylons are built in Denmark by Per Udsen, while the undercarriage is tackled by DAF in the Netherlands, and the wheels by Raufoss in Norway.

European assembly of the F100 engine is handled by the Belgian company Fabrique Nationale, which invested around $35 million in new test cells, machine tools and other equipment. Kongsberg builds the engine fan-drive turbine module in Norway, while Phillips in Holland is responsible for the augmentor nozzle module.

Contracts for avionics are widely scattered throughout the four nations. MBLE (Belgium) has overall responsibility for the APG-66 radar, while Signaal and Oldelft (Netherlands) are responsible for the radar antennae and HUDs respectively. Also involved in HUD work are Marconi Avionics in Britain (the original designer of the unit) and Kongsberg. Danish Industrial Group One (Neselco and LK-NES) supply the fire-control computer, the radar displays are built by Danish company Nea Linberg, and Kongsberg handles the inertial navigation system as well as its other contributions.

The creation of European F-16 production facilities was not an easy task. European industry had earlier built the Lockheed F-104G Starfighter, but the latter aircraft was not in USAF service. Since the F-16 is a front-line US warplane, and would be assembled on both sides of the Atlantic, many procedures had to be agreed, standardized and in some cases made the subject of compromise. In the early days of the YF-16 project, paperwork had been kept to a minimum in order to maintain the pace of the programme, but with the adoption of the F-16 by four NATO nations, Fighting Falcon became what is probably the most complex management task that the US Department of Defense has ever undertaken. In 1977 programme director Brigadier General James Abrahamson described the task he faced as "a management nightmare". More than 3,000 suppliers and subcontractors were involved in the international programme, and even under the 998-aircraft production run originally planned some 20,000,000lb

(9,000,000kg) of raw material and three million individual manufactured items were due to cross the Atlantic.

In an ideal world, the F-16 would not have been committed to large-scale overseas production until the design had been frozen and proven, and until the Fort Worth line had ironed out the inevitable production 'bugs'. In practice, however, the aircraft entered production on a similar timescale in both the US and Western Europe, with production facilities being planned before the design was fully refined or production techniques checked out. Not since the days of the original US ICBM programmes had such pressures been placed on project management.

**Project management**

Since the programme involved contractors in five nations, it was essential to set up procedures under which proposed changes to the design could be jointly discussed and agreed, so that a common standard of hardware would be produced by all of the nations involved. Before components and aircraft could be built, technical standards, acceptance procedures, working practices and even accounting methods had to be jointly agreed. In some cases fundamental differences in procedure and outlook were uncovered.

The US aerospace worker is mobile in outlook, and will tend to 'follow the contracts', working for whatever company needs his services. Two-shift production working is common on large programmes, maintaining production speed and helping to amortize the cost of expensive tooling. In Western Europe, staff are less mobile, with companies placing greater emphasis on long-term workload, and providing greater job security for their employees. Single-shift working is normal, and expensive overtime often frowned upon. It is not uncommon for aerospace plants to shut down completely for anything up to a month during the holiday period.

Such practices may be thought desirable in Europe, but they penalized the performance of the many non-US F-16 contractors. In 1977 it was estimated that European co-production would add over a million dollars to the cost of each F-16 purchased by the NATO air arms. A penalty was also paid in terms of time. As production began, GD estimated the lead time on its Fort Worth line as 24 months, while in the case of the European assembly lines, this rose to 36 months.

In both cases, the end result was increased cost. Unit flyaway price of a USAF F-16 was originally set at $4·55 million in 1975 dollars. The price tag agreed for the NATO aircraft was $6·09 million. Part of this increase was due to R&D levy of $470,000 per aircraft, but the remainder was a reflection of the increased tooling costs and longer lead times.

Methods by which US aerospace suppliers added fixed charges to production costs in order to recover administration and other overhead costs had all been devised to cope with production carried out mostly in the US by US companies. In instances where raw parts might be fabricated in the US, shipped to Europe for finishing, then returned to the US for incorporation within USAF aircraft, normal procedures became distinctly cumbersome.

**Above: F-16 centre-fuselage sections on the production line at Fokker's Ypenburg plant in the Netherlands. These sections show how wing/body blending was used by GD engineers in creating the F-16. The central tunnel houses the F100 turbofan.**

# European co-production

Nordisk

Fokker

SONACA

SABCA

Per Udsen

Fabrique National

GD Fort Worth

Bookkeeping was further complicated by the fact that US procurement procedures dictate that the financial records of companies supplying defence hardware be officially audited, but the European companies involved in F-16 assembly were, not unnaturally, reluctant to allow the US government access to detailed financial data. A compromise was devised under which the individual companies were checked by auditors from their own national governments.

Late in 1976, the smooth running of the programme was disrupted when the USAF decided to standardize on the McDonnell Douglas ACES 11 ejection seat without fully consulting the West Europeans.

The NATO air arms requested a total of 18 changes to the F-16. Seven were subsequently cancelled, six were adopted by all five operators and decisions on five more were deferred. These NATO requests added useful facilities to the aircraft, including:
* improvements to the radar to suppress the effects of sea clutter, and to allow a radar image to be 'frozen' on the display
* navigation update capability
* an altitude-hold facility in the aircraft autopilot
* installation of a radar electro-optical video recorder
* improved anti-corrosion treatment

Despite such problems, and the inevitable political haggling over the distribution of offset work, the programme flowed smoothly during the second half of the 1970s. First European co-production contracts were formally signed in July 1976, and the following October saw the first full-scale development aircraft rolled out at Forth Worth, with the first flight following in December.

**Full-scale production**

The third full-scale development aircraft was used for avionics testing. The radar was delivered two months later, but came with an unexpected bonus – it incorporated a more advanced standard of hardware and software than had been planned – and did not affect the timescale of avionics flight testing.

At the start of 1977 the USAF announced plans to purchase an additional 738 aircraft. Formal authority for full-scale production was given the following October, two months after the first two-seat F-16B flew.

By February 1978 the Belgian production line had opened, followed by

the Dutch line in April. The first F-16 to be delivered to Europe arrived at Gosselies on June 9, 1978, having crossed the Atlantic aboard a USAF C-5 Galaxy. It was used for assembly tests at the SABCA plant. The following month, the first European-built F-16 components – a set of wings – were fitted to a USAF aircraft on the Fort Worth line. The two-way flow of components across the Atlantic had become a reality.

Meanwhile, in the spring of 1978, the US General Accounting Office published a report on the F-16 which drew attention to a number of development problems, including engine malfunctions, structural cracks, minor problems with the radar, and instability at high angles of attack. The report called for the review of the programme and the likely threats which the aircraft would face in service, but pointed out that the problems met to date '... do not seem to be any more severe than those previously experienced in other major systems. And experience with the systems shows that these problems are resolved over time'.

This report attracted some unfavourable publicity for the type, with several knocking reports appearing in print and on TV, but these overlooked the fact that the GAO was to some degree reporting past history. Fixes to many

problems were already at hand.

First flight of a production aircraft from the Fort Worth line took place in August 1978, with the maiden flight of a European F-16 following on December 11, 1978, from Gosselies. This was a two-seat F-16B, and was flown by Neil Anderson and Serge Martin, the latter having spent two weeks on familiarization training at Forth Worth prior to the historic sortie.

Deliveries to the user air arms started in January 1979 when aircraft were delivered from US and European production lines to the 388th TFW at Hill AFB, Utah, and to the FAéB (Force Aérienne Belge, or Belgian Air Force) respectively. In May the first Fokker-built aircraft flew, and four US aircraft completed a four-month series of tests in Europe. A month later the KLu (Koninklijke Luchtmacht, or Royal

Netherlands Air Force) accepted its first F-16s, and in January 1980 deliveries began to the air arms of Denmark, Norway and Israel.

By the end of 1979, the unit flyaway cost of the F-16A was $10·2 million. In numerical terms this may have been far above the $3·0 million originally envisaged back in 1972, but in 1975 dollars was around $4·7 million – well below the USAF 1975 target price of $5·0 million. Until 1980, the F-16 lacked a name. The unofficial use of 'Falcon' resulted in objections by Dassault-Breguet who already used the name for their range of business jets. At a time when the USAF was re-using Second World War nomenclature, the F-16's high performance, long range, bubble canopy and ventral air inlet suggested 'Mustang II' to may observers, but this had been pre-empted by an automobile manufac-

Cockpit side panel

Forward equip. bay structure

Cockpit side panel I & A

Forward equip. bay I & A

Forward inlet assembly

Fuel closure side panel

Aft inlet assembly

Inlet structure

F-1 fuel tank and inlet assembly

Fuel closure side panel

Vertical fin leading edge and antenna

Rudder island

Rudder seals and and inst. parts

Vertical fin skins

Forward section

Vertical fin structure

Forward fuselage structural pickup

Centre section

Aft section

Vertical fin I & A

Forward section

Centre fuselage structure

Aft section

Aft fuselage structure

Fuselage mating

Engine access doors

Dorsal fairing prefit

Centre fuselage I & A

Aft fuselage I & A

Speed brakes and fairings

Engine access doors

Aft/ctr fuselage mate details

Main landing gear

Main landing gear doors

Ventral fins

Radome

Vertical fin panels

Radome details

Dorsal fairings

**Right: The second European F-16 assembly line is at the SABCA plant at Gosselies, Belgium. Deliveries to the air arms of Belgium and Denmark started in January 1979.**

**Below: This flow chart shows the principal structural assemblies of European-built F-16s and identifies the major suppliers. The use of European and American components in aircraft built on both sides of the Atlantic involved an immense administrative effort, and European industrial practices were largely responsible for each locally-built NATO aircraft costing a million dollars more than the USAF equivalent. I & A indicates Integration and Assembly.**

Cockpit structure

Forward fuselage mate

Ejection seat

Canopy

Fwd to ctr fuselage mate details

Forward fuselage and inlet I & A

Nose landing gear door

Nose landing gear

Wing trailing edge panels

Wing box

Trailing edge seals

Wing leading edge flaps

Wing I & A

Wing fuselage fairings

Flaperon seals

Wing flaperons

Engine nozzle fairing

AIM-9 missile launchers

Engine

Horizontal stabilizer

Completed nose radome

Armament

Tail hook

Final assembly

Pylons and fuel tanks

turer. Final choice, made in 1980, was the unimaginative 'Fighting Falcon'.

First phase of the F-16 Operational Test and Evaluation programme was carried out at Hill AFB, Utah, but this was followed by international trials. Nine aircraft took part in the MOTE (Multinational Operational Test & Evaluation) programme, including two from the Belgian and Netherland Air Forces. Six aircraft, plus one of the two reserves and more than 120 personnel, spent six weeks in each of the participating nations during the second half of 1980, so that operating experience could be built up.

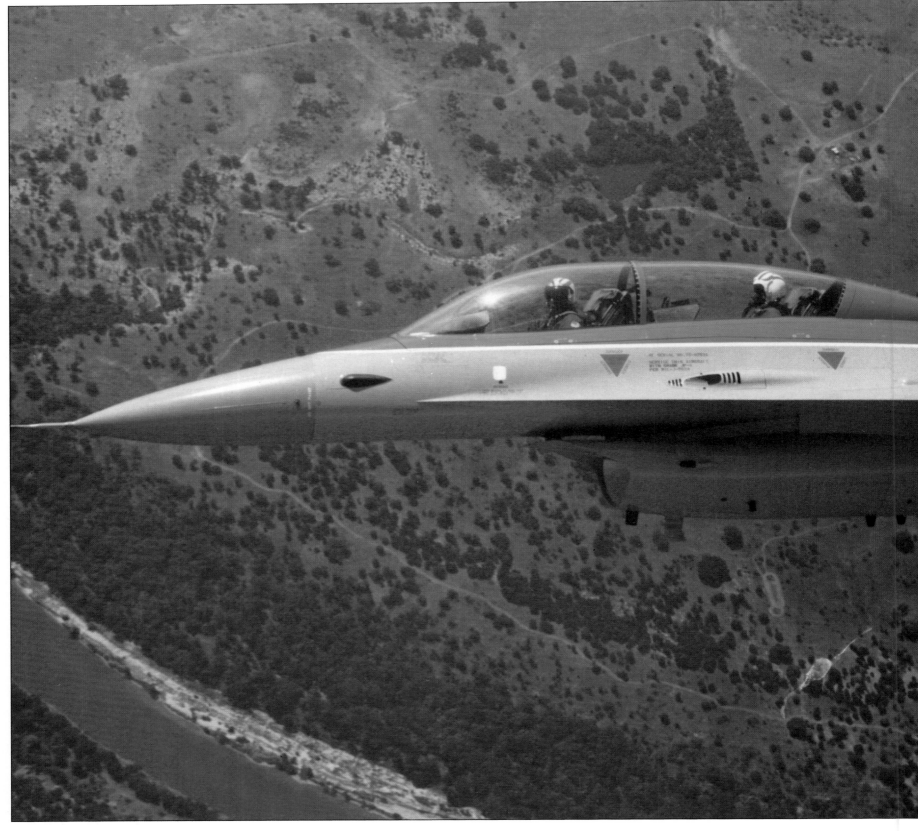

### The F-16/79 export fighter

In the first weeks of 1980 a new shape was given to future US fighter exports when President Carter reversed his 1977 decision that the development of military aircraft specifically for the export market would not be allowed. The guidelines laid down for the proposed FX export fighter called for performance and cost to be between those of the F-5E and the F-16A.

Designs were to be multirole, but optimized for air-to-air combat and with deliberately restricted strike capability. Payload/range performance had to be clearly inferior to that of current front-line types, but deployment and maintenance had to be easier, and the new fighters must not be easily upgradable without US permission. Finally, development of FX fighters was to be a commercial undertaking by the companies concerned, who had to accept all marketing and financial risks. The two obvious candidates were GD with a downrated derivative of the F-16, and Northrop with its new F-5G single-engined member of the Freedom Fighter/Tiger II family.

In order to create the resulting F-16/79 prototype, GD acquired a two-seat F-16B from the USAF in June 1980. The aircraft supplied was 75-0752, one of the original pair of full-scale development F-16Bs. General Electric created a new J79-GE-17X version of this, well-proven single-shaft engine specifically for the project, modifying it to match the F-16 airframe and to give a useful amount of extra thrust.

To keep airframe modifications to a minimum, the J79 installation locates the front face of the engine compressor in a similar location to that of the compressor face in the F100-powered aircraft. Since the GE engine is 18in (46cm) longer than the F100, the rear fuselage has had to be extended aft of the taileron pivot point by an equivalent amount.

The GE turbojet requires a lower airflow than the F100, so GD devised a new pattern of intake. The standard intake had been designed as a single removable component, which made substitution of the new version an easy job. The new unit looks externally similar to the original, but the upper surface extends much further forward, making

an easy recognition feature. This new intake incorporates a fixed compression ramp in its roof, and a bypass valve designed to supply a flow of cooling air to the engine bay.

A steel heat shield weighing almost 2,000lb (900kg) surrounds most of the length of the new engine, and accounts for most of the increased structural weight of the new version. This protects the structure of the aft fuselage from the high level of heat generated by the turbojet. Being a turbofan, the F100 passes relatively cool air from the fan along a duct just below the outer casing, consequently radiating less heat.

### Private venture

Like the rival Northrop F-20, the F-16/79 was developed as a private venture. Total cost of construction and flight test – some $18 million according to a GD estimate – was shared by the airframe and engine manufacturers. Unit flyaway cost was $8.0 million in 1980 prices.

Being only a minimal change from the standard aircraft, the F-16/79 required no new fatigue or other structural testing, and its assembly could be fitted

easily into the normal Fort Worth line. Single and two-seat F-16/79 models were planned, and GD intended to begin deliveries to a customer two years after signing the letter of authorization.

The conversion task was quickly accomplished, and the single F-16/79 prototype flew for the first time on October 29, 1980. By early June of the following year it had clocked up a total of 122 flying hours in 131 sorties, demonstrating a top speed of Mach 2·0 and and altitude of 50,000ft (15,000m) along with 9g manoeuvres. The first flights were naturally for trials purposes, but evaluation flights followed, and by July 1981 28 pilots had flown the aircraft. These included GD personnel and pilots from the USAF, USN and three foreign air forces.

The formal US Department of Defense policy on FX was spelled out in the autumn of 1982, days before Northrop rolled out the F-20 prototype, in a letter from Deputy Defense Secretary Frank Carlucci to Air Force Secretary Verne Orr and Navy Secretary John Lehman. "There are several friends and allies that are now, or soon will be, engaged in the process of modernizing their respective tactical air forces. Only a few can afford first-line fighters, and because of fiscal and other restraints it is important that the United States has alternatives to front-line aircraft available for export.

"The alternative is the FX either as a stand-alone capability or as an element of lo/hi mix. It is clearly in the US national security interest to have our friends and allies equipped with systems that will still be militarily capable in the late 1980s and into the 1990s.

"For this reason, we must selectively but actively encourage the foreign procurement of the FX, not leave this marketing effort just to the manufacturers. Wherever possible and appropriate, your departments will encourage representatives of foreign governments and defence establishments to include the FX in their aircraft modernization plans."

Countries identified as potential FX customers are Bahrain, Egypt, Indonesia, Jordan, Malaysia, Oman, Philippines, Saudi Arabia, Thailand, Turkey and United Arab Emirates. Sales

**Above: Even if the tail markings had been omitted, the extended jet pipe and modified inlets on this two-seater would identify it as an F-16/79.**

**Right: The F-16/79 was developed as an FX-class export fighter, but it remains to be seen whether potential customers will be prepared to accept this deliberately-downgraded design when others are being offered the standard F100-powered aircraft.**

of FX will also be promoted in South America. GD salesmen predicted that up to 20 air arms were potential customers for the F-16/79 and that as many as 1,000 aircraft might be built. Nations briefed on the F-16/79 included Austria, Jordan, Malaysia, Nigeria, Singapore, Taiwan and Thailand.

Austria seemed the most likely launch customer when that nation tested the GD aircraft and the rival Dassault-Breguet Mirage 50 in December 1980. Since the single prototype was unlikely to be available for an overseas sales tour so soon after first flight, GD drew up plans to lease an F-16A from the USAF.

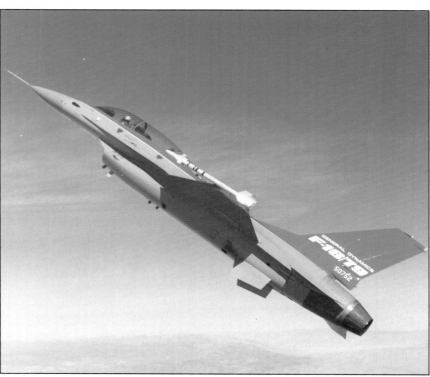

## The F-16/101

While the F-16/79 was taking part in a highly-publicized test programme, GD was also testing a second re-engined version of the Fighting Falcon. On December 19, 1980, GD flew the first F-16 to be powered by the General Electric F110 turbofan. Originally known as the F101 DFE (Derivative Fighter Engine), this was an experimental engine intended to maintain GE design expertise in the field of high-thrust afterburning turbofans and to be a possible new engine for the F-14 Tomcat and F-16.

F-16/101 flight testing went smoothly, all trials objectives being accomplished by May 29 of the following year in 58 sorties and 75 flying hours – 25 hours less than planned. Twelve pilots flew the aircraft during a programme of development trials which included close-support, strike and air-to-air missions. The only major incident which marred this fast-moving and successful test programme was a single dead-stick landing in January 1981 due to a fuel leak.

### Staged improvements

While development of the F-16/79 was being carried out, work on other versions continued. The Fighting Falcon finally achieved Initial Operating Capability (IOC) with the USAF in November 1980, while in January 1981 349 squadron of the Belgian air force became the first F-16 unit to qualify for NATO service in Europe.

A project as large as the F-16 is certain to attract critics. The most common complaint levelled by its detractors, particularly in the earliest stages of the full-scale development programme, was that what started out as a cheap and simple lightweight fighter had grown into a complex and considerably heavier multirole design. To confuse the issue further, a second school of thought claimed that the aircraft and its systems were too simple, and that the Fighting Falcon would have difficulty in operating effectively in Western Europe's often-foul weather.

Simple day fighters of the type originally conceived by the 1972 Lightweight Fighter programme do have a useful operational role, but almost certainly not on NATO's Central Front. The general trend of USAF thinking has been that future version of the F-16 would need more sophisticated systems in order to fight and survive in any 1980s conflict. To create and phase in such new equipment with a minimum of disruption to the Fighting Falcon production programme, the USAF and its NATO allies have devised the Multi-

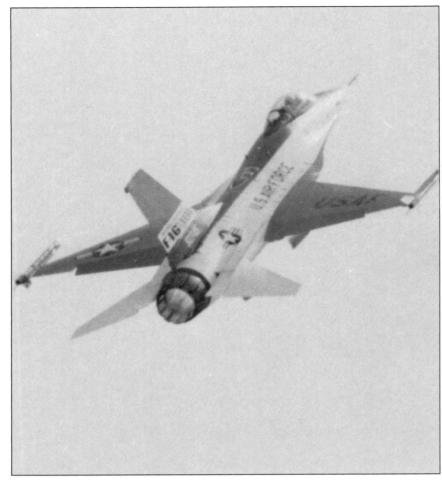

national Staged Improvement Programme (MSIP). This will add improvements in a gradual manner.

The first MSIP Phase 1 aircraft was USAF aircraft no 330, which entered final assembly in the summer of 1981. The NATO consortium introduced the same build standard early in 1982.

Also known as F-16+, the MSIP Phase 1 standard incorporates Engineering Change Proposal 0350, which adds the structural changes and new wiring required by beyond-visual range (BVR) AMRAAM missiles, electro-optical nav/attack systems, internal ECM and other new avionics. A further modification, ECP 0425, involves increasing the size of the horizontal tail, in order to increase the surface's ability to cope with changes of c.g caused by heavy weapon loads. Tail surface area is increased by 30 per cent over the 49sq ft (4·55sq m) of earlier aircraft, empty weight being increased by around 200lb (90kg) as a result. The original component used a titanium pivot shaft and sub-spar, but the opportunity was taken to eliminate this expensive material for the stabilizer. This decision

**Above: First Fighting Falcon to use the General Electric F110 turbofan (formerly the F101 Derivative Fighter Engine) was the F-16/101. The F110 was developed from the F101 powerplant of the B-1 bomber.**

reflected a dramatic increase in the cost of titanium in the late 1970s following the Soviet cutback in exports of the metal.

Under the Pacer Loft programme the European F-16 fleet is being modified to match the USAF standard.

### External differences

The most obvious external sign of Pacer Loft is a grey camouflage finish on the nose radome in place of the earlier black. A new pattern of canopy is physically interchangeable with those on other F-16s, but the remaining improvements are all internal. These include changes intended to cure potential minor problems detected during early service experience. Rain water had been observed accumulating at some locations within the structure, so drainage holes have been drilled in the

forward fuselage area and vertical fin. Maximum takeoff weight is increased from 35,500lb (16,103kg) to 37,000lb (16,783kg), while the all-up weight for 9g manoeuvres has risen from 22,500lb (10,206kg) to 25,300lb (11.476kg).

MSIP Phase 1 prepares the aircraft for Phase 2 – the incorporation of the improved radar, LANTIRN compatible HUD, multifunction head-down CRT displays, uprated environmental control equipment and expanded 'core' avionics including a revised fire-control computer.

Aircraft to be built to this standard are designated F-16C (single seat) and F-16D (two-seat). Target-acquisition and lock-on performance of the APG-66 is improved, and a new movable control stick replaces the earlier unit. If the pilot attempts to fly the aircraft close to the allowable aerodynamic limits, an audible warning is given in his headset.

Two new items of avionics are a data recorder incorporated in the ejection seat in an attempt to ensure that flight-system data survive an accident, and a ground-test panel which checks that secondary power for the flight-control system is available.

Test-flying of some items of the new avionics due to be introduced under MSIP Phase 2 started in 1982. The first Phase 2 aircraft should be assembled on the Fort Worth line in the summer of 1984 and is due to be delivered in July of that year. Production deliveries could start in the following December or early in 1985.

Total cost of F-16C/D all-weather development has reached $5,800 million – two and a half times the previously projected $2,300 million. In order to save money, the first 350 F-16s are not to be updated with MSIP modifications.

MSIP Phase 3 may follow shortly behind Phase 2, depending on the timescale of the new systems. These will include the LANTIRN pods, 30mm gun pod and the Seek Talk secure voice system. Final modifications such as the ASPJ jammer and AMRAAM missile will not enter service until 1985 or later.

While plans for such future versions were being drawn up, the US and European lines continued to deliver the F-16A/B models in ever-growing numbers. In June 1982 the 200th European aircraft was delivered, and the 750th Fighting Falcon to be built was handed over in the following month. Another month brought delivery of the 800th example, and by the end of the year total flying hours of the F-16 had passed the 275,000 mark. By the spring of 1982, the USAF was predicting a total F-16 buy of 2,333 F-16s, having announced

## USAF F-16 improvement plan

plans to buy an additional 945, including 597 enhanced derivative versions.

US military procurement is traditionally handled year-by-year, but the F-16 is one of the few aircraft being purchased under multi-year production plans. This results in real savings to the customer since the manufacturer has the confidence to negotiate with suppliers and subcontractors for larger quantities of components and materials, and to procure long lead-time items for aircraft to be built in the later stages of the contract. When this scheme was mooted in 1982, GD pointed out that 120 aircraft could be delivered per year under a multi-year contract for the level of funding which would pay for only 96 under annual procurement methods.

The 1984 US defence budget allocates a total of $2,300 million to F-16 procurement in 1984, and $3,200 million in 1985, which will allow production to run at 120 aircraft per year. This may seem a long way from the original concept of a 'cheap' fighter, but if spent on F-15 Eagles the same money would buy only half that number.

**Right: Jet pipes of the F110-powered (left) and standard F100-powered (right) versions of the F-16.**

**Below: Fighting Falcon has now flown with the GE J79 turbojet, GE F110 (formerly F101 DFE) turbofan and the standard P&W F100 turbofan.**

## Current F-16 production delivery schedule

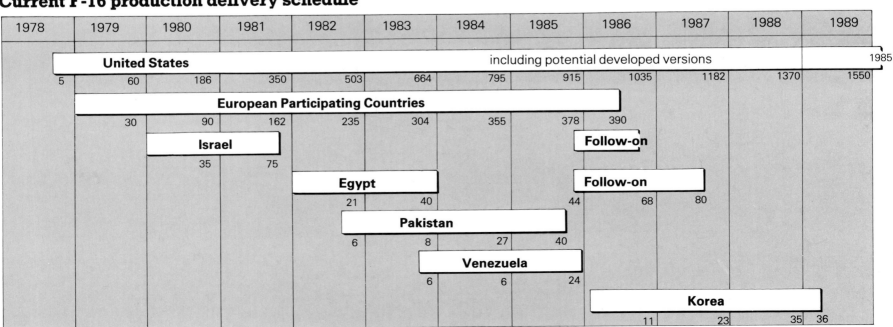

| | 1978 | 1979 | 1980 | 1981 | 1982 | 1983 | 1984 | 1985 | 1986 | 1987 | 1988 | 1989 |
|---|---|---|---|---|---|---|---|---|---|---|---|---|
| **United States** | | | | | | | | including potential developed versions | | | | 1985 |
| | 5 | 60 | 186 | 350 | 503 | 664 | 795 | 915 | 1035 | 1182 | 1370 | 1550 |
| **European Participating Countries** | | | | | | | | | | | | |
| | | 30 | 90 | 162 | 235 | 304 | 355 | 378 | 390 | | | |
| **Israel** | | | | | | | | | Follow-on | | | |
| | | | 35 | 75 | | | | | | | | |
| **Egypt** | | | | | | | | | Follow-on | | | |
| | | | | | 21 | 40 | | 44 | | 68 | 80 | |
| **Pakistan** | | | | | | | | | | | | |
| | | | | | 6 | 8 | 27 | 40 | | | | |
| **Venezuela** | | | | | | | | | | | | |
| | | | | | | 6 | 6 | 24 | | | | |
| **Korea** | | | | | | | | | | | | |
| | | | | | | | | | 11 | 23 | 35 | 36 |

# Structure

In designing the structure of the F-16, General Dynamics engineers never lost sight of the fact that the end product must be easy to produce. Wherever possible, the attractions of advanced constructional methods such as chemical milling and exotic materials such as titanium and carbon-fibre composites were rejected. Without compromising the performance of the aircraft, the GD team created hardware which would eventually be assembled on three production lines by Belgian, Dutch and US workers, using components built to a common standard by sub-contractors on both sides of the Atlantic.

Fighting Falcon may be a high-performance aircraft of advanced aerodynamic form, but in designing its structure the GD engineers eschewed wherever possible sophisticated constructional techniques and materials. The USAF wanted an inexpensive fighter, so a modularized and simplified structural design was adopted.

Despite the aircraft's high performance, some 80 per cent of the structure is manufactured from aluminium alloy. A little less than 8 per cent is made from steel, composites account for less than 3 per cent, and titanium for a mere 1.5 per cent. Around 60 per cent of the structural parts are made from sheet metal, while less than 2 per cent require chemical milling.

The weight savings resulting from the use of advanced technology such as relaxed stability and wing/body blending are very significant, resulting in an empty weight some 1,300lb (590kg) less than would have been the case with a more conventional design. During full-scale development, GD estimated the cost of the F-16 airframe structure as $60 per lb, so this reduction in theory reduced airframe costs by around $80,000.

The development of a military aircraft is often a long saga of ever-increasing takeoff weight. This problem had dogged the F-111, the previous Fort Worth design, but in engineering the production F-16 the GD team maintained rigorous control over weight growth. Between April 1975 and January 1978 the takeoff weight increased by just over 5 per cent from 22,197lb (10,068kg) to 23,357lb (10,595kg), but more than half of this 'fat' reflected increased operational capability, producibility or maintainability.

**Fatigue tests**
In parallel with the flight-test programme a series of ground fatigue trials were carried out on the fifth development airframe. A test rig set up in a hangar at Fort Worth used more than 100 hydraulic rams to apply stress to an instrumented airframe, simulating the loads imposed by takeoff, landing and combat manoeuvring at up to 10g. By the summer of 1978, this airframe had clocked up more than 16,000 hours of simulated flight in the rig. These tests were carried out at a careful and deliberate pace which sometimes lagged behind schedule.

As the tests progressed, cracks developed in several structural bulkheads. News of this problem resulted in hostile comments in the media, but GD pointed out in its own defence that the cracks had occurred not in flying aircraft but on ground test specimens. If the risk of such cracks during development testing was not a real one, a company spokesman remarked to the author at the time, no-one would be willing to pay for ground structural test rigs. GD redesigned the affected components, thickening the metal, and installed metal plates to reinforce existing units.

Built up from three major sub-sections – nose/cockpit, centre and aft – the fuselage is based upon conventional frames and longerons. The forward manufacturing break point is just aft of the cockpit, while the second is located forward of the vertical fin.

Combined with advanced aerodynamics and the low sfc of the F100 turbofan, the increase in fuselage internal volume created by wing/body blending accounts for the GD fighter's impressive range performance. Some 28 per cent of the weight of a loaded F-14 is fuel, while the equivalent figure for an F-16 is 31 per cent.

Anyone who has seen an F-16 under-

**Above: Production aircraft on the Fort Worth assembly line. At this stage the canopy and radome still have protective coverings.**

going an engine change cannot help noticing the effect of wing/body blending on the aircraft's internal fuel capacity. Visiting the Fort Worth flight line in 1977, the author was shown an engineless F-16 – one of the development aircraft on the flight line was undergoing an engine change. Looking up through the tail and out through the air inlet, his first reaction was "Where do you keep the fuel?". At first sight it seemed impossible for so much kerosine to be stowed in the limited space which remained.

Wing/body blending was carried out in three dimensions. Seen from the front or rear of the aircraft, the wing gradually blends in cross section with the fuselage, making it impossible to define where the wing ends and the fuselage begins. This blending is varied lon-

**Below: Belgian ground crew prepare an F-16 for flight. The avionics technician needs no steps or ladder in order to work on the radar.**

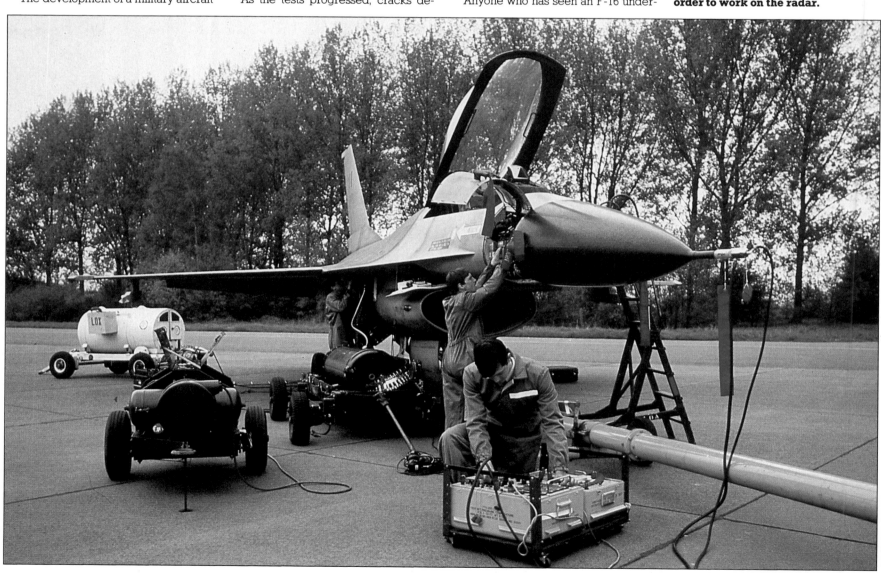

gitudinally in order to 'tailor' the cross-sectional area distribution.

In planform, the wing leading edge also blends with the fuselage thanks to the leading-edge strakes. At high angles of attack, these create vortexes which maintain the energy of the boundary air layer flowing over the inner section of the wing. Wing root stalling is thus delayed, and directional stability maintained. Vortex energy also provides a measure of forebody lift, reducing the need for drag-inducing tail trim. Graphic proof of the existence of these vortexes may be seen during tight turns if local condensation results in a 'con-trail' from the strakes. At air shows, the aircraft has been flown with smoke generators whose plumes have clearly shown the trailing vortexes. And by keeping the inner-wing boundary layer energized, the strakes allowed a reduction in wing size, aspect ratio and weight – a saving of around 500lb (227kg) in structural weight.

The combination of wing/fuselage blending and variable camber resulted in several advantages, including the additional space provided in a location close to the centre of gravity for internal fuel, avionics and other systems. Without this feature, the F-16 would have been about 5ft (1.5m) longer and the structure some 570lb (259kg) heavier.

Gradually increasing thickness of the wing in the region of the wing root resulted in a stiffer wing than would have been possible with a conventional design. Stiffness was increased by the fact that the lift-increasing manoeuvring flaps allowed a smaller wing of reduced span to be used. The wing structure itself incorporates five spars and 11 ribs. Upper and lower wing skins are one-piece machined components.

### Aerodynamic performance

Fineness ratio of the F-16 configuration is lower than the ideal for supersonic flight, but transonic drag is minimized. In conventional designs, wing lift normally falls off at high angles of attack, but the F-16 obtains a useful amount of body lift.

The leading-edge manoeuvring flap and trailing-edge flaperon can be moved at up to 35deg/sec to match Mach number and angle of attack. Maximum speed of movement is matched to the aircraft's ability to respond to changes in pitch, so that flaps and aircraft attitude are always matched.

By shaping the wing aerofoil to match aerodynamic conditions, the moving flaps reduce drag, maintain lift at high angles of attack, improve directional stability, and minimize buffeting. The latter qualities are useful during tight turns in air combat, or while 'jinking' at low level to confuse hostile air defences. The wing is only around 1.5in (3.8cm) deep at the point where the

leading-edge rotary actuator is installed, so the design of this component was a significant challenge.

In the spring of 1982 actuator failures caused the USAF temporarily to ground all F-16s which had exceeded 200 hours of operational flying – 240 of the 400 F-16s in service at that time – for inspection of the wing leading-edge flap. A routine inspection had revealed signs of excessive wear in the actuation mechanism which controls the position of the leading-edge manoeuvring flap. More than 40 aircraft required repair, the remainder being returned to service once this component had been inspected – a process which took around five man-hours per aircraft. As an interim solution pending a definitive 'fix', aircraft were re-inspected every 100 hours.

The vertical stabilizer has a multi-

spar and multi-rib structure made from aluminium alloy as is the unit's top cap, but the skins are fabricated from graphite epoxy. Also located under the rear fuselage is a runway arrester hook.

The original pattern of horizontal stabilizer is being replaced by a larger component under the MSIP Phase I programme, details of which are given later in this chapter. Inboard of each are the air brakes. Stowed in the horizontal position when not in use, these are of the split type, the upper and lower sections of which open through an angle of 60deg.

The main undercarriage units retract forwards into the lower fuselage, and the large doors were found to offer a good – although unconventional – mounting location for Sparrow or Sky

**Above: By early 1979 the production line in GD's mile-long assembly building was picking up speed. The aircraft nearest the camera was delivered to the USAF in May.**

Flash radar-guided missiles. The nose gear is located aft of the intake, so that debris or other foreign objects thrown up by the wheel will not be ingested into the engine air intake.

The location of the intake is certainly unconventional, but wind tunnel tests showed that the ventral location is subject to minimal airflow disturbance over a wide range of flight conditions and aircraft manoeuvres, since the forward fuselage tends to shelter it from the effects of aircraft manoeuvres. At an angle of attack of 25deg, for example, the air flows into the intake at an angle of only 10deg.

**By altering the settings of the leading and trailing-edge flaps the F-16 flight-control system can match the camber of the wing to flight conditions, thus maximizing wing efficiency.**

Takeoff during ground roll
−2° / 20°

Takeoff after liftoff
15° / 20°

Reflexed for high speed cruise
−2° / −2°

Maximum manoeuvre configuration
25° / 0°

Approach configuration
15° / 20°

Landing at wheel spin up
−2° / 20°

Critics who predicted in the mid-1970s that the F-16 would suffer a high incidence of engine damage due to FOD (foreign object damage) have been proved wrong. The lower edge of the intake lip is 38in (97.5cm) above the ground, high enough to minimize the chances of small objects or fragments of debris being sucked in. A study of the limited clearance between intake and runway surface on types such as the Boeing 707 (inboard engines) and 737 airliners might have suggested that all would be well, but such obvious comparisons were often overlooked during the wave of F-16 knocking carried out by some 'experts' as Europe was tooling up to build the type.

Conventional wisdom suggests that the complexities of variable geometry are mandatory in an intake for use at Mach 2. Like the creators of the earlier Saab-Scania J37 Viggen, however, the GD engineers ignored the rule book and devised a simple fixed-geometry unit incorporating a boundary-layer splitter plate. This was designed as a single assembly to make future updating easy (a feature later found useful during the development of the turbojet-powered F-16/79 variant). A more traditional variable-geometry intake assembly had been designed, but at present it seems unlikely see service.

In order to reduce the number of spare parts which F-16 units must hold, some components are designed to be interchangeable between port and starboard. These include the horizontal tail surfaces, wing flaperons, 80 per cent of the main landing gear components, and many of the actuator units.

Like any aircraft, the Fighting Falcon is only as good as its pilot. Aircrew assigned to the F-16 are housed in the most sophisticated cockpit that the technology of the early 1970s could devise. Later fighters such as the F/A-18 Hornet may have more advanced electronics, but no other aircraft in the Western world – and probably in the entire world – has the combination of reclining seat and sidestick controller used in the F-16.

Research suggested that a pilot's tolerance could be increased by the use of a reclining seat whose back was tilted at angles of up to 65deg. GD engineers compromised by adopting a tilt of 30deg and by raising the pilot's knees and legs. In terms of providing extra pilot tolerance to high-g manoeuvres the cockpit layout was probably a success, but the disadvantages of such a configuration seem to have prevented its being used in later designs. Studies carried out by other manufacturers suggest that the raised leg position markedly reduces the panel area which may be used to house displays and instruments.

Good all-round visibility is provided by a canopy whose forward and centre sections are made from a single piece of polycarbonate. An impressive item of plastics engineering, this suffered from 'teething troubles' early in its development. The transparency was required to withstand the impact of a 4lb (1.8kg) bird at 350kt, and passed initial tests with flying colours. Following some minor problems with the canopy protective coating on the YF-16, the USAF modified the latter, but the revised

## General Dynamics F-16 Fighting Falcon cutaway

1 Pitot tube
2 Glassfibre radome
3 Planar radar scanner
4 ILS glidescope aerial
5 Scanner drive units
6 Radar mounting bulkhead
7 ADF aerial
8 Forward electronics equipment bay
9 Westinghouse AN/APG-66 digital pulse doppler radar electronics
10 Forward identification light, Danish and Norwegian aircraft only
11 Radar warning antenna
12 Cockpit front pressure bulkhead
13 Instrument panel shroud
14 Weapons systems fire control electronics
15 Fuselage forebody strake fairing
16 Marconi-Elliot wide-angle raster-video head-up display (WARHUD)
17 Side stick controller (fly-by-wire control system)
18 Cockpit floor
19 Frameless bubble canopy
20 Canopy fairing
21 McDonnell-Douglas ACES II zero-zero ejection seat
22 Pilot's safety harness
23 Engine throttle
24 Side console panel
25 Cockpit frame construction
26 Rear pressure bulkhead
27 Ejection seat headrest
28 Seat arming safety lever
29 Cockpit sealing frame
30 Canopy hinge point
31 Ejection seat launch rails
32 Rear electronics equipment bay (growth area)
33 Boundary layer splitter plate
34 Fixed geometry engine air intake
35 Lower UHF/IFF aerial
36 Aft retracting nosewheel
37 Shock absorber scissor links
38 Retraction strut
39 Nosewheel door
40 Forward position light
41 Intake trunking
42 Cooling air louvres
43 Gun gas suppression nozzle
44 Air conditioning system piping
45 Forward fuselage fuel tank, total system capacity 1,072·5 US gal (4,058 litres)
46 Canopy aft glazing
47 Starboard 370US gal external fuel tank (1,400 litres)

48 Forebody blended wing root
49 Upper position light and flight refuelling floodlight
50 Fuel tank bay access panel
51 Rotary cannon barrels

52 Forebody frame construction
53 M61 Vulcan, 20mm rotary cannon
54 Ammunition feed and link return chutes
55 Ammunition drum, 500 rounds

56 Ammunition drum flexible drive shaft
57 Hydraulic gun drive motor
58 Leading-edge flap control shaft
59 Hydraulic equipment service bay
60 Primary system hydraulic reservoir
61 Leading-edge manoeuvre flap drive motor
62 TACAN aerial
63 No 2 hydraulic system reservoir
64 Leading-edge flap control shaft
65 Inboard pylon
66 Pylon fixing

67 Wing centre pylon
68 Triple ejector bomb rack
69 MK 82 500lb (227kg) bombs
70 Oldelft Orpheus reconnaissance pod, Netherlands aircraft only
71 Infra-red linescan
72 Camera ports
73 Reconnaissance pod pylon adaptor, centre line fixing
74 SUU-25E/A flare launcher
75 AN/ASQ aircraft instrumentation system data link transmitter
76 Outboard wing pylon
77 Missile launch shoe

78 AIM-9L Sidewinder air-to-air missile
79 Advanced medium range air-to-air missile (AMRAAM)
80 Aluminium honeycomb leading-edge flap construction
81 Starboard navigation light
82 Static dischargers
83 Fixed trailing edge section

84 Multi-spar wing construction
85 Integral wing fuel tank
86 Starboard flaperon
87 Fuel system piping
88 Access panels
89 Centre fuel tank bay access panel
90 Intake ducting
91 Wing mounting bulkheads
92 Universal air refuelling receptacle (UARSSI)
93 Engine compressor face

94 Pratt & Whitney F100-PW-100(3) afterburning turbofan engine
95 Jet fuel starter
96 Engine accessory gearbox, airframe mounted
97 Gearbox drive shaft
98 Ground pressure refuelling receptacle

design promptly failed its final qualification tests.

This failure triggered off a re-examination of the canopy design and test procedures, and studies of alternative canopy designs. A newer and heavier pattern of canopy was developed in order to ensure adequate resistance to bird strikes. The final design meets all USAF requirements, and offers a level of visibility which must leave MiG-21 and Mirage III pilots drooling with envy. Its high 'bubble' profile may result in some penalty in terms of supersonic drag, but the F100 engine has more than enough thrust to cope. Visibility from the cockpit covers a full 360deg in the horizontal plane, and from 15deg down over the nose through the zenith and back to directly behind – a total of 195 deg. Sideways visibility extends down

**Above: A technician examines the forward undercarriage leg of a Belgian Air Force F-16. Note the inlet strut for increased rigidity**

to a depression angle of 40deg. The polycarbonate is 0.5in (1.3cm) thick, but its optical quality is high, and the curved surfaces offer minimal distortion of the outside view.

The ejection seat selected for production F-16s was the McDonnell Douglas ACES II (Advanced Concept Ejection Seat) used on the F-15 Eagle. This is a rocket-powered unit with a vectored-thrust STAPAC pitch-control system. Mounted beneath the seat, STAPAC consists of a small vernier rocket motor with a thrust of 235lb (107kg) and a 0.3sec burn time. As the seat leaves the cockpit, a gas generator spins up a pitch-rate gyro. This is uncaged and the vernier motor lit. The latter normally has its thrust axis aligned with the nominal centre of gravity of the seat and its occupant: should the seat pitch forwards

or backwards due to aerodynamic forces or a low or high centre of gravity, the STAPAC vernier will be vectored to apply a corrective force.

ACES II offers zero-zero performance. From a stationary aircraft parked on the ground, it will lift to a height of more than 100ft (30m) and carry rearwards by at least 50ft (15m). Built-in survival equipment includes emergency oxygen, a URT-33C radio beacon, a liferaft and a rucksack.

The Multinational Staged Improvement Plan (MSIP) approved in February 1981 brought in a series of improvements developed under Engineering Change Proposal ECP350. This included modifications to the structure and wiring of the wings to allow the carriage of AMRAAM, the provision of hardpoints on the intake sides to carry

99 Flaperon servo actuator
100 Rear fuselage frame construction
101 Rear integral fuel tank
102 Main engine mounting suspension link
103 Upper UHF/IFF aerial
104 Fuselage skin plating
105 Starboard side-body fairing
106 Fin root fillet
107 Flight control system hydraulic accumulators
108 Anti-collision light power supply unit
109 Starboard tailplane (increased area 'big tail')
110 Tailplane surfaces interchangeable port and starboard

111 Graphite-epoxy skin panels
112 Fin construction
113 Aluminium honeycomb leading-edge panel
114 Steel leading-edge strip
115 VHF communications aerial
116 Anti-collision light
117 Tail radar warning antennae
118 Aluminium honeycomb rudder construction
119 Rudder servo actuator
120 Radar warning power supply

121 Brake parachute housing, Norwegian aircraft only
122 Tail navigation light
123 Electronic countermeasures aerials, port and starboard (ECM)
124 Fully variable exhaust nozzle
125 Nozzle flaps
126 Split trailing edge airbrake, upper and lower surfaces
127 Airbrake hydraulic jack

128 Port tailplane (increased area 'big tail')
129 Static dischargers
130 Graphite-epoxy tailplane skin panels
131 Corrugated aluminium sub-structure
132 Hinge pivot fixing
133 Tailplane servo actuator
134 Nozzle sealing fairing
135 Fueldraulic nozzle actuators
136 Afterburner tailpipe
137 Rear fuselage bulkheads
138 Rear engine mounting
139 Aft position light
140 Port side-body fairing
141 Runway arrester hook
142 Ventral fin, port and starboard
143 Port flaperon
144 Flaperon hinges
145 Aluminium honeycomb flaperon construction
146 Static dischargers
147 Fixed trailing edge section
148 Port AIM-9L Sidewinder air-to-air missiles

149 Missile launcher shoe
150 Wing tip launcher fixing
151 Port navigation light
152 Outboard pylon fixing rib
153 Multi-spar wing construction
154 Centre pylon attachment rib
155 Wing centre pylon
156 MK 84 2,000lb (908kg) low-drag bomb
157 Leading-edge manoeuvre flap
158 Leading-edge flap rotary actuators
159 Integral wing fuel tank
160 Inboard pylon fixing
161 Wing attachment fishplates
162 Landing/taxiing lamp
163 Main undercarriage shock absorber strut
164 Mainwheel leg strut
165 Retraction strut
166 Mainwheel door
167 Forward retracting mainwheel
168 Port underwing fuel tank, 370US gal (1,700 litres)
169 Centre line external fuel tank, 300US gal (1,378 litres)
170 Electro-optical forward looking infra-red pod (EO-FLIR)
171 Laser target designator pod (LAST)
172 LAU-3/A rocket launcher, 19 × 2·75in (6,98cm) ground attack rockets
173 Westinghouse AN/ALQ119-1 electronic suppression system radar jamming pod (ESM)
174 Snakeye, 500lb (227kg) retarded bomb
175 GBU-10C/B 2,000lb (908kg) laser guided bomb

**McDonnell Douglas ACES II ejection seat**

A Environmental sensor pitots
B Recovery parachute container
C FLCS data recorder
D Recovery parachute risers
E Emergency oxygen bottle
F Emergency oxygen pressure gauge
G Inertia reel knob
H Ejection control safety lever
I Radio beacon switch
J Survival kit (under seat pan)
K Ejection handle
L Restraint emergency release handle
M Lap belt and survival kit attachment
N Emergency oxygen fitting

the LANTIRN electro-optical system, and wiring and structural provisions in the cockpit for the LANTIRN HUD, head-down multi-function displays and other improved avionics.

Load capacity of the centre wing pylons rises from 2,500lb (1,135kg) to 3,500lb (1,590kg). Other modifications prepare the aircraft for the ASPJ ECM system and make provision for a radar altimeter. Control logic of the aircraft environmental control system was also modified to increase system efficiency.

## MSIP I modifications

Although the USAF does not expect to take delivery of the new avionics items until the end of 1984, it programmed the associated structural and wiring modifications into the production line in 1981 under the MSIP I programme. These changes added approximately 200lb (90kg) to aircraft weight.

A new horizontal tailplane of increased area is the most obvious external evidence of the MSIP I modifications. Introduced by Engineering Change Proposal 425, this provides the greater control force required to cope with heavy munition loads. When large ordnance loads are carried, aircraft centre of gravity is moved further forward, increasing stability and making the F-16 more difficult to manoeuvre.

The revised tail is easier and less expensive to produce, since its structure does not incorporate titanium. The rising cost and poor availability of this metal led GD to redesign the tailplane spar and pivot in aluminium as part of ECP 425, resulting in a cost saving of 20 per cent. Corrugated aluminium alloy, mechanically fastened to the carbon-fibre skins, replaced the earlier filling of aluminium honeycomb, which was bonded into place. The finished

stabilizer is thicker than the original component, but thanks to the increased span the thickness-to-chord ratio remains unchanged. At the same time, the need for a braking parachute led GD to modify the vertical fin to allow the fitting of this item should customers so desire.

Wherever possible, the design makes maintenance easy. Ground crew working on the F-4 Phantom had to cope with 510 individual lubrication points, 281 fuel line connections, more than 900 individual electrical connectors and 294 avionics units. In the case of Fighting Falcon, lubrication points have been cut to 84, and fuel line connections to 90, while the avionics technicians have only 52 units to deal with. The number of connectors remains high at 841, but these now incorporate silicone grommets, so are easier to service than earlier patterns of connector which were potted (sealed) with rubberized compound after assembly. As a further aid to maintenance, around 60 per cent of the surface of the aircraft is removable, the Fighting Falcon design incorporating 228 access doors. Only four tools are required to open these, and 80 per cent of the aircraft systems are accessible without stands.

## Old technology

Some technology from earlier General Dynamics fighters – the Convair F-102 Delta Dagger and F-106 Delta Dart – was used in the F-16 programme. Tests have shown that a fuel tank sealant designated AF-10 Scotchweld which was used on these 1950s designs had a better performance and required less maintenance than the more modern polysulphide rubber-like compounds now in use, and offered cost savings of 25 per cent or more. During tests on F-16 centre-fuselage and aft-fuselage

tanks, the older type of sealant successfully withstood the standard 5psi (0.35kg/sq cm) air-pressure test.

The most drastic structural modification which the Fighting Falcon has undergone was that imposed by the 'cranked-wing' F-16XL project, whose new delta wing uses a planform originally proposed for use on supersonic airliners. Developed in conjunction with NASA's Langley Research Centre, it is intended to offer low drag at high subsonic and supersonic speeds without losing low-speed manoeuvrability. It is of multispar delta design with a leading edge sweep angle varying from 50deg to 70deg. Area is 120 per cent greater than that of the basic wing, while wing weight rises by 2,600lb (1,179kg). Weight is reduced by the use of carbon

composite materials for the upper and lower skins. Had these been made of aluminium alloy, the wing would have been some 600lb (272kg) heavier.

During the conversion work, the length of the aircraft fuselage was extended by 56in (142cm) This was accomplished by adding two new fuselage sections at the junctions between the three main fuselage sub-assemblies. One 30in (76cm) section is located at the front split point, and a 26in (66cm) section at the rear. This increase in fuselage and wing size allowed internal fuel capacity to be increased by 82 per cent. The latter factor dramatically increases the payload/range performance of the modified aircraft. The F-16XL is intended to carry twice the payload of the F-16 40 per cent further.

**Above: Single-seat version of the F-16XL**

**Below: The modular design of the basic F-16 fuselage allowed new sections to be spliced in to create the longer fuselage of the F-16XL.**

**Below right: The first F-16XL was a single-seat aircraft powered by a P&W F100 turbofan and with a wing area increased by 120 per cent.**

F-16 maintenance is facilitated by the provision of 228 access panels.

Above: A USAF technician removes an access panel from the wing of a 428th Tactical Fighter Squadron F-16 during Exercise Cope Elite 1981.

Right: Although the wing planforms of the F-16/79 (lower) and F-16XL are very different, the fuselage displays a high degree of commonality.

## F-16 Fighting Falcon detail comparisons

1. Nose section of the F-16B and D trainers.
2. F-16/AFTI with intake-mounted canards, and dorsal spine containing avionics and instrumentation.
3. Plan view of F-16A and C single-seat versions.
4. Single-seat F-16XL with cranked arrow wing.
5. Tailplane fitted to early production aircraft.
6. Definitive tailplane of increased area.
7. Rear fuselage of F-16/79.
8. Norwegian aircraft have a modified tail fairing which houses a braking parachute.

# Powerplant

**John Boyd's concept of Specific Excess Power called for the F-16 to have a high thrust-to-weight ratio, which in turn required an engine of superlative performance. Such a powerplant was already available in the form of the F100 turbofan devised by Pratt & Whitney for the earlier F-15 Eagle programme. The F100 could deliver the thrust, but its development and deployment stretched US engine technology to the limits. Despite a series of teething troubles, however, the USAF and P&W persisted with development work until all problems were solved.**

Development of the Pratt & Whitney F100 turbofan started in August 1968, when the USAF awarded development contracts to P & W and General Electric for engines suitable for use in the planned FX fighter – later to become the F-15 Eagle. In view of the high thrust-to-weight ratio planned for the new fighter, the resulting engines would have to push the technology of the time to its limits. P&W faced the daunting task of developing a powerplant producing 25 per cent more thrust per pound of weight than the contemporary TF30 turbofan used in the F-111, and twice that of the J75 turbojet used in the F-105 Thunderchief and F-106 Delta Dart.

Both companies built and ran demonstration engines whose light weight, high thrust and low fuel consumption put them well ahead of previous designs. The P&W engine was selected by the USAF for further development, contracts being awarded in 1970. Two versions were originally planned – the F100 for the USAF and the F401 intended to power later models of the US Navy's F-14 Tomcat, though the latter was cancelled when the USN was ordered by the Department of Defense to cut back the size of the planned F-14 fleet.

The F100 is an axial-flow turbofan with a bypass ratio of 0.7:1. It has two shafts, one carrying a three-stage fan driven by a two-stage turbine, the other carrying the ten-stage main compressor and its two-stage turbine. The completed engine is 191in (4.85m) long and, 34.8in (0.88m) in diameter at the inlet, and weighs 3,068lb (1,392kg).

New technologies used in the F100 included powder metallurgy. Instead of forming some metal components in the traditional manner, P&W reduced the raw material to a powder. This could be heated and formed under high pressure to create engine components better able to tolerate the high temperatures planned for the F100 core.

Operating temperature of the F100 turbine was far above that of earlier engines. Successful turbojets of earlier vintage, such as the GE F85 which powers the F-5E, or the GE J79 used in the F-4 and F-104, had turbine inlet temperatures of around 1,800deg F (982 deg C). P&W had achieved figures of just over 2,000deg F (1,093deg C) in the TF30 turbofan, but to meet the demanding requirements of the F100 specification involved temperatures of 2,565deg F (1,407deg C).

Use of such advanced technology resulted in an engine capable of providing the high levels of thrust required by the F-15 and F-16. Maximum thrust is normally described as being 'in the 15,000lb (6,800kg) thrust class' when running without afterburner, and 'in the 25,000lb (11,340kg) class' at full augmentation.

Normal dry (non-afterburning) rating is 12,420lb (5,634kg), rising to a maximum of 14,670lb (6,654kg) at full Military Intermediate rating – the maximum attainable without afterburning. Specific fuel consumption (sfc) – the amount of thrust produced for each pound of fuel burned per hour – is 0.69 at normal rating, 0.71 at Military Intermediate. At full afterburning power, the F100 develops 23,830lb (10,809kg) of thrust at an sfc of 2.17. At this rating, the engine swallows an impressive 860lb (390kg) of fuel per minute.

By the time the F-15 Eagle was ready for its first flight in July 1972, the F100 had completed most of its test programme, meeting 23 out of 24 critical 'project milestones'. Between February and October of the following year, a series of turbine failures dogged attempts to complete the 150-hour run-

ning trial which formed part of the formal Qualification Test. The latter was the most punishing series of tests to which any US military jet engine had ever been subjected, according to P&W. It included 30 hours of running at a simulated speed of mach 2.3, and 38 hours of running at a simulated Mach 1.6.

Following completion of this test, the F100 was subjected to a further series of intensive trials, including 150 hours of running at over-temperature conditions, and a long series of Accelerated Mission Tests. Conducted on the ground, but designed to simulate the stresses of operational service, these were intended to build up running time and detect potential problems. None of these was serious enough to delay the start of F-15 production, and the first

**Above: A USAF crewman at Kunsan Air Base in South Korea fuels an F-16. Engines in the F100 thrust class require large amounts of fuel.**

**Below: At full afterburning thrust, the F100 consumes more than 800lb of fuel per minute. This aircraft is from the 8th TFW, based at Kunsan.**

aircraft were delivered to the USAF in November 1974. The F-15 powerplant is designated F100-PW-100 by the company and JTF22A-25A by the USAF.

Despite the obvious merits of the P&W F100 turbofan, including the fact that this engine had already been selected for use on the F-15, GD carried out many studies of the smaller General Electric YF101 engine. The P&W engine was very much a product of late 1960s thinking – a high bypass ratio turbofan offering good and economical performance at its military (dry) rating – while the GE powerplant was a more modern engine with a much lower bypass ratio. Only a small amount of air was ducted past the core in this design, which GE had dubbed a 'leaky turbojet'.

In many ways, the GE engine was more conservatively designed, emphasis having been placed on reliability rather than ultimate performance. GE personnel made no secret of their view that the P&W engine was pushing the technology of the time close to the limits.

Factors considered by GD during the engine evaluation were the weight of the rival powerplants plus the fuel needed for cruise, combat and reserve. The YF-16 design mission included a 500nm cruise to the target area at high subsonic speed, acceleration to combat speed using maximum afterburner, a period of combat in full afterburner involving sustained turns and supersonic and subsonic speeds, then a return to base with a 20-minute sea-level reserve.

### Weight calculations

Combined fuel and engine weight for this mission was calculated to be 7,882lb (3,575kg) using a single F100, or 10,234lb (4,642kg) for twin YF101 engines. Two YF101 engines plus installation would weigh 1,024lb (464kg) more than would be the case with a single F100, while an extra 1,328lb (602kg) of fuel would have to be carried. Using the twin GE installation, the F-16 design team would have come up with an aircraft with a mission weight of 21,470lb (9,739kg) instead of the 17,050lb (7,734kg) promised by the P&W engine.

If aircraft weight were kept constant, an F100-engined YF-16 would have a 70 per cent greater mission radius than a twin-YF101 design, GD estimated. Some 90 per cent of this increase came in roughly equal proportions to the lower engine weight and fuel load required by an F100-powered design, the remainder to reduced drag and airframe weight.

The lower bypass ratio and lighter weight of the F100 installation produced dividends in many areas, GD estimated. Under static conditions at sea level, a pair of YF101 'leaky turbojets' would produce an extra 5,200lb (2,359kg) of thrust, but at Mach 1.2 the turbofan

offered an additional 7,500lb (3,402kg). The difference at 30,000ft (9,000m) and Mach 2 was less marked, but the P&W engine still offered a useful 2,850lb (1,293kg) of extra thrust.

In cruising flight, the big turbofan offered a thrust-to-weight ratio seven per cent better than that of the two YF101 engines, and with a 25 per cent lower fuel flow. At 30,000ft and Mach 2, fuel flow was more evenly matched, but thrust-to-weight ratio was dramatically improved. The P&W engine would consume 6.5 per cent less fuel, but produce a 41 per cent higher thrust-to-weight ratio.

In one instance the F100 turned out to have too much thrust. The residual thrust from an idling F100 was 670lb (304kg) – too high for F-16 operations on icy runways. In theory, this residual thrust could have sent a lightly-loaded

F-16 moving at speeds of up to 50kt, rather too much for taxying. A test programme using the second YF-16 showed that the engine could be adjusted to give a lower idling speed, reducing the taxying speed to a more acceptable figure.

USAF hopes that the F100 would be a mature powerplant by the time the F-16 entered service were dimmed by a series of technical and operational problems. Strikes at two major subcontractors delayed the delivery of engines, while service experience showed that the F100 was wearing out twice as fast as had been predicted. By the end of 1979 the USAF was being forced to accept engineless F-15 airframes, and by the spring of the following year some 30 were in storage. A massive effort by P&W brought the delivery situation under control, but for

**Above: To clear the F100 for service, the engine was subjected to the most demanding series of ground tests ever devised for a USAF powerplant.**

a long time the F-15 and F-16 fleets remained short of engines.

A modification introduced into the fuel pump of the F100 created problems for the F-15 early in that aircraft's career. In cruising flight, cavitation could begin in the pump, badly damaging the pump vanes. The solution adopted on the F-15 was simple – revert to the original design. In the case of the F-16, a pump failure would be more serious, so Sundstrand developed an

**Below: Specifically developed for use in the F-16, the F100-PW-200 has additional anti-stagnation-stall features for single-engine safety.**

alternative dual-element pump for this aircraft. This runs at a lower speed, and should one section fail, the other can continue to deliver fuel at a lower rate.

The electronic engine control unit uses the fuel as a coolant. This technique for obtaining 'free' cooling led to problems when the F-15 first entered service. During training missions at Luke AFB, aircraft sometimes had to wait for 45 minutes or more before takeoff, with engines running at idle settings. This gradually heated the mass of fuel in the Eagle's tank to the point where it was no longer cold enough to cool the engine control unit. Given the high temperature of the desert environment at Luke, the unit could not radiate the excess heat away, so tended to overheat, resulting in engine overspeed problems and turbine failures.

Early operational and durability problems with the F100 during the late 1970s were largely overcome by modifications, plus improvements in materials, maintenance and operating procedures. Production of spare parts was accelerated, and field maintenance teams were increased in size.

Part of the problem lay in the fact that the USAF had underestimated the number of cycles which engines aboard such high-performance types as the F-15 and F-16 would actually undergo. (A cycle is defined as the temperature variation experienced in a mission from engine start to maximum power and afterburner, then back to the lower settings used for landing.) In 1977 the service estimated that each engine would undergo 1.15 cycles per flight hour, but in practice the rate was 2.2 for the F-15 and 3.1 for the F-16.

At one time, designers had assumed that the most arduous duty which a jet engine had to face was running for long periods at high power levels. By the late 1960s, research had shown that this was simply not the case. Many failures were due to this type of running, but others were created by the heating and cooling resulting from an engine being run up to high power then throttled back.

Technicians dubbed this 'low-cycle fatigue', but had to admit that it was difficult to measure. To aid the design of future engines such as the F100, estimates were made of the average number of thermal cycles to which an engine would be exposed per flying

hour. Unfortunately for the F100 programme, these estimates were wrong. In practice, engines were being subjected to far more thermal cycles than the designers had allowed for.

Paradoxically, the additional stress which the engines were receiving was largely due to the F-15 and F-16 being such good aircraft. Given the high manoeuvrability of their new mounts, pilots were flying in a manner not possible on earlier types, pushing the aircraft to high angles of attack and making full use of the extended performance envelope. In the heat of a dogfight, the throttle setting would be changed much more often than on earlier fighters. All this spelled hard work for the engine.

### Air combat demands

The F-16 places more strain on the engine than does the F-15, since the Fighting Falcon is used in the demanding air-combat role. P&W studies showed that throttle excursions placed a greater strain on the engine than long runs at a constant setting. Studies involving instrumented test aircraft gathered data on the number of throttle movements and the amount of afterburner use which test F-16s were clocking up, and the company carried out a series of accelerated mission tests to clear the F100 for use in the GD aircraft.

Critical components such as first-stage turbine blades showed signs of distress, condemnation rate during repair being 60 per cent instead of the predicted 20 per cent. Maximum gas temperature was reduced to conserve component life, while R&D funding was concentrated on improvements to reliability rather than increasing thrust. Despite these problems, the F-15 had a better engine-related safety record by the end of the 1970s than any other USAF fighter at a comparable point in its service career.

Another problem which was to dog the F100 during the first years of its service career was stagnation stalling. The compressor blades in a jet engine are of aerofoil section, and, like the wing of an aircraft, can be stalled if the angle at which the airflow strikes them exceeds a critical value. Powerplant stalls are occasional occurrences in most jet engines, particularly in the early stages of development, but the F100 was to prove excessively vulner-

able to stagnation stalling during its first few years of operational service.

Turbofans are prone to a particularly severe type of stall from which recovery is not possible. As the flow of air through the compressor is disturbed, the engine core looses speed, while the combustor section of the engine continues to pass hot gas to the turbine, causing the latter to overheat. If this condition is not noticed, the turbine may be damaged.

Experience with the F-15 showed that in the event of a mild hard start, the pilot might not notice that a stall had occurred, as the loss of acceleration on the twin-engined aircraft was often not sharp enough to indicate to the pilot that one engine had failed. Without a check on the temperature gauge, low-pressure turbine entry temperature could reach the point where damage might occur. To avoid this problem, an audible-warning system was devised for the Eagle. This is not needed on the Fighting Falcon, since a stall of the single engine produces an immediate loss of acceleration.

Some stagnation stalls were found to be due to component failures, but most were linked with afterburner problems. The latter usually took the form of 'hard starts' – virtually mini-explosions within the afterburner. In some cases the afterburner failed to light on schedule; in other instances the burner extinguished. In either event, large amounts of unburned fuel were sprayed into the jetpipe, creating a momentary build-up of fuel. When this was ignited by the hot efflux from the engine core, a pressure pulse was created – the aerospace equivalent of a car backfiring.

### Deliberate hard start

A reporter from *Aviation Week* gave this account of a deliberately induced hard start on a test stand: "The force of the auto-ignition was sufficient to rock the heavily sound-insulated concrete test building. A large gout of flame at the afterburner exhaust was seen on the closed-circuit colour-television system." The pressure in the afterburner resulting from a hard start sent a shock wave back up through the fan duct. When this reached the front section of the engine, it could cause the fan to stall, or, in the worst case, both. It was sometimes possible for a series of stagnation stalls

**Above: Dwarfed by the bulk of the McDonnell Douglas KC-10A Extender, an F-16 connects the 'flying boom' to its receptacle during tests of the new tanker/cargo aircraft.**

to occur, with each resulting in the afterburner hard start needed to trigger off another.

Stagnation stalls usually took place at altitude and at high Mach numbers, but rarely below 20,000ft (6,100m). Normal recovery method was for the pilot to shut down the engine and allow it to spool down. Once the tachometer showed that engine rpm had fallen below the 50 per cent mark, the throttle could safely be reopened to the idle position, and the F100 would carry out its automatic relight sequence. The F-16 is fitted with a jet-fuel starter, but from a height of 35,000ft (10,700m) a pilot would probably have enough time to attempt at least three unassisted starts using ram air. Critical factor in restarting the engine after a stagnation stall is the low-pressure turbine-inlet temperature. This must fall to 450deg F (232deg C) before the engine can be restarted.

Several modifications were devised to reduce the frequency of stagnation stalls. The first approach taken was to try to prevent pressure build-ups in the afterburner. A quartz window in the side of the afterburner assembly allowed a flame sensor to monitor the pilot flame of the augmentor. If this went out, the flow of fuel to the outer sections of the burner was prevented.

When the F100 engine-control system was originally designed, P&W engineers allowed for the possibility that ingestion of efflux from missiles might stall the engine and a 'rocket fire' facility was designed into the controls. When missiles were fired, an electronic signal could be sent to the unified fuel control system which supplies fuel to the engine core and to the afterburner. The angle of the variable stator blades in the engine could be altered to avoid a stall, while the fuel flow to the engine was momentarily reduced, and the afterburner exhaust was increased in area to reduce the magnitude of any pressure pulse in the afterburner.

Tests had shown that the 'rocket fire' facility was not needed, but P&W engineers were able to use it as a means of preventing stagnation stalls. Engine

**Above: A night-time engine test at the Pratt & Whitney plant. The F100 is in full afterburner, and the nozzle has been fully opened to allow the hot exhaust gases to expand.**

shaft speed, turbine temperature and the angle of the compressor stator blades are monitored on the F100 by a digital electronic engine control unit, which normally serves to 'fine-tune' the engine throughout flight to ensure optimum performance.

By monitoring and comparing HP spool speed and fan exhaust temperature, the engine control unit is able to sense that a stagnation stall is about to take place, and send a dummy 'Rocket Fire' signal to the unified fuel control system to initiate the anti-stall measures described above. At the same time, a second modification to the fuel control system reduces the afterburner setting to zone 1 – little more than a pilot light – in order to help reduce pressure within the jetpipe.

In an attempt to prevent any pulses coming forward through the fan duct from affecting the core, P&W engineers devised a modification known as the 'proximate splitter'. This is a forward extension to the internal casing which splits the incoming airflow from the engine compressor fan, passing some to the core of the engine and diverting the remainder down the fan duct, past the core and into the afterburner. By closing the gap between the front end of this casing and the rear of the fan to just under half an inch, the engine designers reduced the size of the path by which the high-pressure pulses from the burner had been reaching the core. Engines fitted with the proximate splitter were test-flown in the F-15, but this modification was not embodied in the engines of production Eagles, whose twin engines made the loss of a single engine less hazardous.

When it first flew, the F-16 seemed almost free of stagnation stall problems, but while flying with an early-model F100 engine, one of the YF-16 prototypes did experience a stagnation stall,

**Right: Ready for refuelling during a 4,350 mile (7,000km) flight across the United States intended to simulate a transatlantic deployment, an F-16 approaches the boom of a KC-135.**

though this occurred outside the normal performance envelope. Three incidents were noted later during flight tests at high angles of attack. All took place at Edwards AFB during low-speed flight tests at high altitude. The first production aircraft to experience a stagnation stall was an FAéB aircraft operating near the limits of the performance envelope. The pilot was able to restart the engine and landed safely.

Given the amount of development work, the stagnation stall problem was soon mastered, although never completely eliminated. To suit the F100 for the single-engined F-16, the USAF decided to adopt the modifications already fitted to the engines of the F-15, plus the proximate splitter.

The F-16 powerplant is designated F100-PW-200 by the manufacturer, JTF22A-33 by the USAF. It weighs 54lb (24.5kg) more than the original version fitted to the F-15, and incorporates a back-up fuel-control system and a modified cooling system for the control system, which has a hydromechanical back-up.

The improvement in reliability was dramatic. Back in 1976, the F-15 fleet experienced a stagnation stall rate of 11–12 per 1,000 flying hours. By the end of 1981 this had dropped to 1.5 per 1,000 hours thanks to the modifications to the fuel control system and nozzle. Engines fitted to the F-16 fleet (and incorporating the proximate splitter) had an even lower rate – 0.15 per 1,000 hours.

The need for greater engine reliability in the single-seat F-16 has forced the USAF to be cautious when problems emerge. In the summer of 1980, for example, engines in USAF, European and Israeli service were inspected following the discovery of a broken control cable in the wreckage of an aircraft which crashed at Hill AFB during a low-level training flight. This was seen as a precautionary measure for the single-seat aircraft: for the twin-engined F-15 spot checks were deemed sufficient.

Efforts are under way to reduce further the smoke output of the F100 as part of a planned component-improvement programme. For example, the combustor has been modified to increase the velocity of the airflow in its front end. This results in improved mixing of air and fuel and leads to more complete combustion and less residual smoke.

Traditional engine-servicing techniques involve replacing critical components at the end of a statistically calculated lifetime. This often results in components being removed and scrap-

**Below: A pilot of the 429th Tactical Fighter Wing carries out a pre-flight inspection of his Fighting Falcon's ventral intake.**

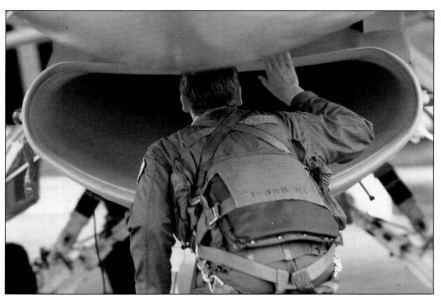

| F100/J79 comparative data | F100 | J79 |
| --- | --- | --- |
| Manufacturer | Pratt & Whitney | General Electric |
| Type | turbofan | turbojet |
| Bypass ratio | 0.71 | – |
| Dry thrust (1b/kg) | 14,670/6,654 | 11,810/5,357 |
| Afterburning thrust (1b/kg) | 23,830/10,810 | 18,730/8,496 |
| Weight (1b/kg) | 3,835/1,740 | 3,847/1,745 |
| Thrust:weight ratio (with afterburning) | 6.2:1 | 4.87:1 |
| Turbine inlet temperature (deg F/deg C) | 2,565/1,149 | 1,810/821 |
| Number of components | 31,100 | 22,000 |
| Maintenance man hours/flight hour (1978) | 4.2 | 1.7 |

ped while still perfectly serviceable, giving good safety margins, but at a high cost to the operator. The USAF now wants engine designers to develop parts with greater tolerance to crack damage so that these may be left in the engine until inspection by non-destructive test (NDT) methods shows that cracks are starting to develop and a replacement is needed. Life-cycle costs may be cut by up to 60 per cent.

The service's Damage Tolerant Design (DTD) programme involved both Pratt & Whitney and General Electric, and focussed much of its attention on the F100. One of the programme's first achievements was a new pattern of F100 fan disc having five times the life of the original component. Key design elements under DTD are high quality control of the raw material, and the avoidance of shapes and configurations which cause stress concentrations – sharp radii, for example.

### New components
The USAF plans to begin testing engine discs currently under development as part of the DTD programme in 1984, and hopes to fit these into operational engines before the end of that year. By 1985 or 1986 the F100 may be fitted with second and third-stage turbine blades and vanes manufactured using a single-crystal technique. Although more expensive than components made from traditional materials, these will probably have a lifetime at least twice that of current vanes and blades.

The USAF was the first F100 user to take advantage of a warranty scheme offered by P&W in 1980, whereby the company undertook to repair or replace certain high-pressure turbines unserviceable as a result of wear or mechanical failure at no extra cost to the USAF. Engines covered by the deal were from production lot IX and were due for delivery between February 1981 and January 1982.

To qualify for free treatment, faulty engines would have to have carried out less than 900 equivalents of the TAC engine operating cycle (about two years of normal use) or have developed the fault within three and a half years of delivery. If the HP failure had caused secondary damage to the engine, P&W

undertook to cover costs up to 75 per cent of that of a new engine.

### The F-16/79
The General Electric J79 turbojet seemed an obvious choice as powerplant for the planned FX export version of the F-16 in view of that engine's widespread use. Production of the J79 in the US ended in 1979 after a total of 13,686 had been built for use in the B-58 Hustler, F-104 Starfighter and F-4 Phantom. Licence production in Japan ended early in 1980, but the powerplant remained in production in Israel for the Kfir fighter.

The J79 is a single-shaft axial-flow turbojet with a 16-stage compressor and three-stage turbine. The former incorporates variable inlet vanes and six stages of variable stators. The combustor is of cannular type with ten burners. For the F-16/79 project, GE engineers devised a new version designated J79-GE-17X, and incorporating a new feature which the company called Combat Plus. When this is demanded by the pilot, fuel flow to the engine is slightly increased, while the exhaust nozzle closes slightly. The net result is to increase exhaust gas temperature by around 100deg F (56deg C), producing several hundred pounds of extra thrust.

Combat Plus cannot be used at all times. The engine must be running in full afterburner, compressor inlet temperature must not exceed 15deg F (–9 deg C), and certain combinations of low altitude and high speed would place excessive strain on the engine casing due to excessive internal pressure resulting from the high airflow involved.

The exact level of thrust increase created by Combat Plus varies depending on engine operating conditions. On a ground test bed, maximum thrust in full afterburner rises from 17,900lb (8,119kg) to more than 18,700lb (8,482kg). In a high altitude test chamber, maximum thrust with Combat Plus rises to 20,840lb (9,453kg) at Mach 2/35,000ft (10,700m) operating conditions.

Ratings when installed in an airframe will be further modified by the inlet configuration, but for many flight conditions GE claims that the uprated J79 will result in minimal performance loss. The superiority of the F100 is very marked in terms of fuel consumption, however. At military (non-afterburning) ratings the turbojet burns more fuel than the turbofan, although this is not a problem in the range-constrained FX mission. When the afterburner is lit, the difference in fuel consumption is minimal, according to GE.

Another modification required to match the J79 to the F-16 airframe was the addition of a transfer gearbox designed to mate with the airframe-mounted gearbox on the F-16 which drives electrical generators and hydraulic pumps. The engine also incorporates safety features originally devised for use on single-engine installations such as the F-104 Starfighter and Kfir.

Three development engines were built. The first was used to carry out 60 hours of formal Preliminary Flight

Rating Tests, running for five hours under simulated Mach 2 conditions. The second was supplied to GD for use in the F-16/79 prototype, while the third acted as a back-up.

Although the F-16/79 has not yet entered service, and by mid–1983 had yet to attract an order, the future of the Combat Plus feature of the J79 may be assured. Development of Combat Plus was originally begun as a means of improving the performance of the F-4, but some development work was carried out in the mid–1970s for Israel. The latter work led to further developments by Israeli engineers, and the IDFAF is reported to be considering its use in the J79-IAI-J1I powerplant of Kfir.

### The F-16/101
In the search for an alternative engine for the F-14 Tomcat and the F-16, the US Department of Defense awarded General Electric a $100 million contract to build five F101 Derivative Fighter Engines (DFE) for flight test. The first engine reached full power on December 30, 1979, the first day of ground testing. During the following month it clocked up 60 hours of running at all power levels. It was designed to be a direct replacement for the F100 in the F-16 airframe, and to be installed in the Tomcat by means of extended fore and aft mountings.

As well as serving as an alternative powerplant, the F101 maintained General Electric design expertise in high-thrust engines, ensuring that two com-

**Above: Final adjustments are made to an F100 turbofan at the Pratt & Whitney works.**

**Left: Technicians manoeuvre an F100 into the second FSD aircraft. The multi-flap articulated nozzle is seen here in the open position used when the afterburner is lit. When dry thrust is selected, the nozzle closes to a narrower diameter.**

panies would be able to offer designs for future engines of this performance level.

By the autumn of 1980 the F101 had completed 430 hours of accelerated mission testing – the equivalent of 1,000 hours of F-16 flying. Since testing had begun, maximum thrust had fallen by less than two per cent, while specific fuel consumption in afterburning mode had increased by just over one per cent. The engine was stripped down for examination, found to be in good con-

dition, then rebuilt to undergo testing intended to simulate 1,000 hours of flying in the F-14.

### F100 developments

Pratt & Whitney are continuing research into new engines based on the F100 and its technology. During a series of tests carried out in late summer of 1982, the company ground-tested an F100 fitted with a two-dimensional nozzle. Rectangular in cross-section, this is a convergent/divergent design featuring

movable upper and lower surfaces which could be used to vector the thrust. This design was developed under a USAF contract, and while no production application is planned, the new nozzle could be used in a modified F-16 or F-15.

Angles of up to 20deg were demonstrated, but P&W is confident that the design would be good for up to 30deg. Coupled with the use of thrust reversing, this technique could greatly increase the agility of current aircraft, and

could cut the take-off run to 1,200ft (366m) or less. Earlier attempts to design axisymmetric nozzles with vectoring and thrust-reversing have resulted in complex and heavy units which paid a high penalty in thrust loss. The latest P&W design could be offered as an add-on modification weighing only a few hundred pounds to the standard F100 gas generator section.

Using experience gained from the F100 programme, P&W was able to begin development of the PW1120 afterburning turbofan. Based on the core of the earlier engine, this is a low-risk development with 60 per cent commonality, but it incorporates a new low-pressure compressor and turbine, and a simplified afterburner. Operating temperature has been slightly reduced, and the PW1120 has a slightly lower thrust-to-weight ratio – 7.25:1 instead of 7.9:1. The PW1120 is 20in (50.8cm) shorter than the F100 and 7in (17.8cm) narrower in diameter. First application to be announced was the planned Israel Aircraft Industries Lavi fighter.

# Avionics

**Advanced aerodynamics and a high thrust-to-weight ratio are not enough to make an advanced fighter. Without its complex payload of avionics 'black boxes', Fighting Falcon would not be able to search for and locate its targets under typically poor European weather conditions, or confuse hostile ground-based or airborne radars. And without the assistance of the complex fly-by-wire flight-control system, the F-16 pilot would probably be unable to cope with the inherent instability of his aircraft. With these systems installed, however, a basic lightweight fighter becomes a formidable multirole combat aircraft.**

Like most US military aircraft, the F-16 carries a comprehensive suite of avionics. The basic installation in the F-16A/B is already greater than many proponents of the original Lightweight Fighter scheme may have envisaged, but this reflects the combat environment of the 1980s rather than any desire by GD or the USAF to 'gold plate' the aircraft. Under the MSIP and F-16C/D programmes even more systems will be added to improve all-weather capability. Some critics attack the Fighting Falcon as being over-complex, but the original concept of a simple day fighter is no longer suited to Western European operations.

Integration of the F-16 avionics makes extensive use of the MIL-STD-1553 multiplexed databus – a significant step forward in avionics design. The significance of computer languages and interfaces may seem obscure, but the complexity of modern warplanes makes standardization of these as important as the standardization of more tangible objects such as fixings, fastenings, connectors and weapon attachment points.

Traditional methods of avionics integration involved the use of bulky and expensive bundles of electric wiring for the distribution of signals and data. Multiplexing is a technique under which various equipments share a common electrical connection on a time-sampled basis – the electronic equivalent of time-sharing an apartment. If the number of times per second during which a signal has access to the electrical connection – databus – is sufficiently high compared with the rate at which that signal may change, the end result will be as acceptable as a fixed piece of wire. Lightweight digital switching electronics may therefore be substituted for heavy and bulky cabling.

### Avionics standardization

By specifying an agreed 'code of conduct' for using the databus, MIL-STD-1553 greatly reduces the electronic interfacing problems experienced in earlier digital avionics systems, in which each manufacturer selected his own independent software (computer programs and instructions) as he saw fit.

GD was an enthusiastic supporter of avionics standardization, and all avionics for the F-16 were developed using a common interface and computer language. For the avionics improvements planned as part of the MSIP programme, the company standardized on the latest version of MIL-STD-1553, the Jovial computer language and a new standard interface for stores and stores-management systems.

### The APG-66 radar

Primary target-detection sensor of the F-16 is the Westinghouse APG-66 radar. As originally conceived, the F-16 would have carried only a simple search set, probably similar in performance to that in the Northrop F-5E. Some individuals in the Department of Defense even suggested the use of a basic range-only unit with a fixed antenna.

Experience during the Vietnam War had shown how enemy aircraft could avoid detection by flying close to the ground, where the clutter experienced on normal pulse radars could hide them from observation. The need to have 'look-down' radar capability forced the adoption of a pulse-Doppler radar, but the traditional high complexity and cost of such equipment made the design of the much smaller APG-66 a difficult task.

In order to carry out a radar-controlled interception, an aircraft requires data on the bearing of the target and its range. Bearing can be measured by means of a highly-directional antenna giving good angular discrimination, but range data can most easily be obtained by pulsing the radar transmitter on and off again at a rate known as the pulse-repetition frequency (PRF). In the simpler types of radar equipment, sufficient time is allowed for one pulse to travel out to the target, be reflected, and return to the radar before the next pulse is transmitted. Engineers describe such radars as low-PRF sets.

Until the 1960s, airborne radars were almost blind when attempting to look downwards to detect low-flying aircraft. The latter were able to hide in the clutter produced by the strong radar echo from the terrain background against which they were being viewed.

**Above: Westinghouse engineers install line-replaceable units in a development APG-66 radar to be test-flown in an F-4 Phantom.**

**Below: Marconi Avionics' holographic HUD begins flight trials in the front cockpit of an F-16B. The large combiner glass gives the unit the wide field-of-view needed for use with LANTIRN.**

By the 1960s a new source of microwave power known as a travelling-wave tube (TWT), along with the use of digital signal processors, allowed the creation of pulse-Doppler radars with a good look-down performance.

The use of stable and coherent (phrase-related) pulses from a TWT allows the radar to measure the Doppler shift in the radar returns from the target – the tiny change in frequency caused by target motion relative to the signal source. Using this technique, the relative velocity of the target against the terrain background allowed the wanted target signal to be extracted from the massive background returns. This technique is known as pulse-Doppler radar.

TWT transmitters cannot match the high levels of power available from the magnetron transmitters used in low-PRF radars, so the designers were forced to use high PRFs in order to illuminate the target with sufficient power. Since each pulse would be transmitted before the previous pulse had completed the round trip out to a distant target and back, each pulse had to be electronically 'labelled' by a low-frequency modulation at the time of transmission.

### Medium PRFs

The range data obtained by processing the labelled pulses is of low accuracy, and high PRFs are also poor at detecting targets whose closure rate is low. In the 1970s, therefore, designers of airborne radar turned to medium PRFs. These allow traditional methods of ranging to be used at most combat ranges, while still allowing pulse-Doppler techniques to be used for look-down operation.

Since the PRFs best suited to range measurement are different to those effective against low closing-rate targets, a practical design of medium-PRF set has to switch rapidly from one PRF value to another. This made the design of hardware able to carry out pulse-Doppler signal processing virtually impossible. The solution lay in the use of software-controlled digital signal processing. By making the characteristics of the filter dependent on a computer program (software) rather than physical components (hardware), the designers could contrive near-instantaneous reconfiguration of the filter to match each PRF waveform used by the radar. The first radars to use medium PRFs and digital signal processors were the Hughes APG-65 in the F-15 Eagle and the L.M. Ericsson PS-46/A in the Viggen JA37 intercepter.

**Below: The final FSD aircraft was temporarily fitted with a mock-up of an enlarged nose able to house the APG-65 radar used in the F/A-18.**

Development contracts for the F-16 radar were awarded to Hughes and Westinghouse, and both companies test-flew prototypes in a competitive evaluation before Westinghouse was awarded the contract for what became the APG-66. The specification was very demanding, calling for a medium-PRF pulse-Doppler set capable of being installed in the modestly-sized nose section of the Fighting Falcon.

The set was initially optimized for the air-to-air role, but air-to-surface modes were also requested soon after the fly-off. To minimize possible delays and cost increases, some compromises in air-to-ground performance were accepted. At high altitudes, for example, radar ground-mapping performance is lower than would have been possible with an antenna optimized for this role.

The APG-66 used in the F-16A/B is a medium-PRF radar (typically 10 to 15kHz). It operates in I/J band and incorporates a 'flat-plate' planar array antenna. Sixteen operating frequencies are available within the band, and the pilot may select between any four. Total weight is 296lb (134kg), and the set occupies a volume of 3.6cu ft (0.1cu m). A mean time between failures of 97 hours has been demonstrated.

Radar operating modes may be selected by the pilot using the throttle, sidestick controller or radar control panel. Like most modern sets, the APG-66 is designed so that all the controls needed during air combat are located

**Above: Primary sources of nav/ attack data for the F-16A pilot are the HUD (top) and square CRT display (between the pilot's knees).**

on the control stick and throttle. When the set is tracking a target, the range scale is switched automatically to reduce pilot workload.

Primary air-combat mode is Downlook, which provides clutter-free indication of low-flying targets. Fighter-sized aircraft may be detected head- or tail-on at ranges of more than 30nm (34.5 miles/55.6km). If the target is flying at a higher altitude than the Fighting Falcon, the pilot may select Uplook mode, gaining a useful 33 per cent increase in detection range.

**Below: Performance of the APG-66 radar against typical aircraft targets: the figures for the Soviet aircraft are estimates based on results with US types. Ranges obtained in look-up mode are better than those in look-down mode – in the latter case the set must carry out sophisticated signal processing to distinguish between the target and unwanted radar reflections from the ground.**

**Opposite: All controls needed during combat are mounted on the sidestick controller (top) and throttle (below). The Dogfight/MSL override switch on the latter can be set to the 'Dogfight' position to select radar Air Combat mode.**

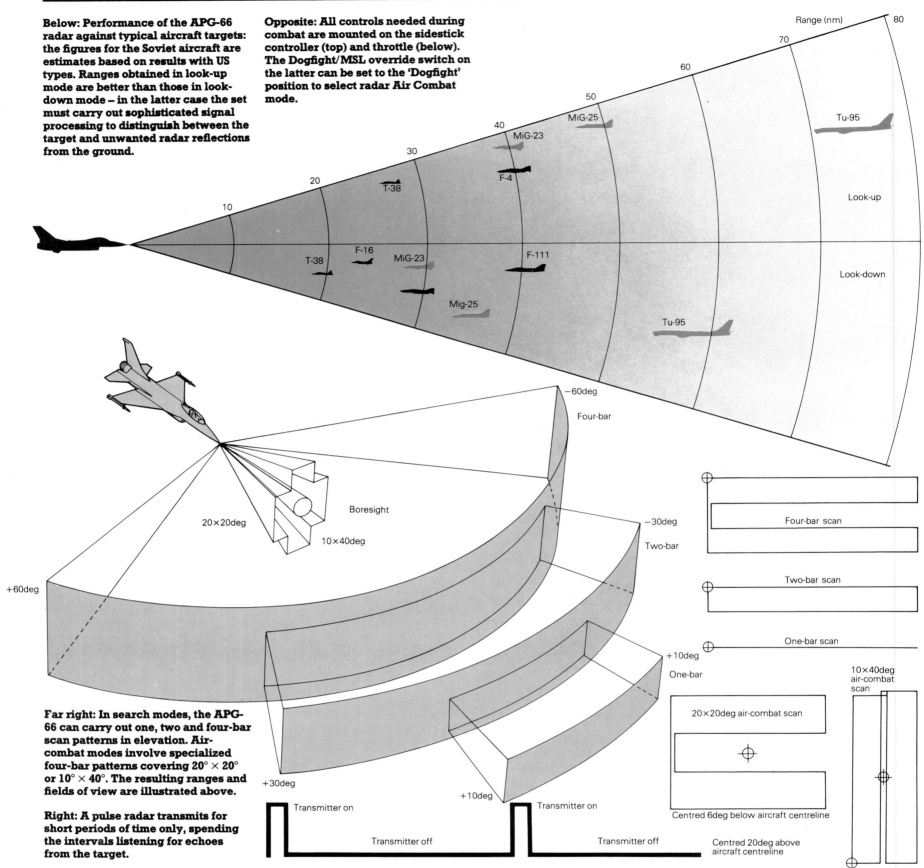

**Far right: In search modes, the APG-66 can carry out one, two and four-bar scan patterns in elevation. Air-combat modes involve specialized four-bar patterns covering 20° × 20° or 10° × 40°. The resulting ranges and fields of view are illustrated above.**

**Right: A pulse radar transmits for short periods of time only, spending the intervals listening for echoes from the target.**

Four modes are available for air-to-air combat. In the Dogfight mode, selected by means of a throttle-mounted switch, the radar automatically scans a 20deg × 20deg field. If the pilot can see the target in his HUD, and the range is less than 10nm, the radar will automatically lock on. If high-g manoeuvres are to be carried out, the area to be searched can be altered to a 40deg × 10deg pattern.

If faced with several closely-spaced targets, the pilot can press the Designate button on his sidestick controller. The radar will then operate in a slim narrow-beam mode, and by manoeuvring his aircraft the pilot can place the beam on to the required target. When he releases the Designate switch, the radar will acquire and track the chosen victim.

Slewable air-combat mode can give the Fighting Falcon pilot the edge during combat manoeuvres. A cursor-control button on the throttle grip allows the scan pattern to be moved to anticipate target manoeuvres. This is particu-

larly useful when both aircraft are manoeuvring in the vertical plane.

Seven modes are provided for air-to-surface use. Air-to-ground ranging is automatically selected during continuously-computed impact point (CCIP) and dive-toss attacks, measuring the slant range to a designated point on the ground.

**CCRP attacks**

Continuously-computed release point (CCRP) attacks use the set's ground mapping modes. Real-beam ground mapping gives a plan position indicator (PPI) display at 10, 20, 40 or 80nm range, and scan widths of plus or minus 10deg, 30deg or 60deg. This image may be used for navigational updates, the location and detection of ground targets and for direct or offset weapon delivery.

Dedicated sea-surface search modes may be used in the maritime role. Sea 1 is a frequency-agile mode for use against stationary or moving vessels in up to sea state 4, while Sea 2 uses a narrow Doppler notch to detect moving

targets in higher sea states, and may also be used to indicate moving targets on land.

Beacon mode also uses a PPI display format. It may be used in conjunction with ground-located radar beacons to take navigation fixes or to carry out offset weapons delivery. In the air-to-air role, this mode is used to locate flight refuelling tankers by interrogating their beacons.

Several auxiliary methods of presenting imagery may be used in these PPI modes. If Freeze mode is selected, the radar carries out a final scan, the image of which is 'held' on the display, following which the radar transmitter is turned off so that the aircraft cannot be detected by passive means. A moving symbol on the display continues to indicate aircraft motion. Expanded-beam real map mode provides an optional ×4 magnification on all PPI modes. The pilot selects the 'patch' to be expanded from anywhere within the radar's scan and range limits.

Highest definition of ground features

is given by a special Doppler beam sharpened mode. Usable when the set is ground mapping at ranges of 10 or 20nm, this provides a further ×8 magnification over that in expanded-beam real map mode. Since this mode relies on the processing of Doppler shift, it is only available at angles between 15deg and 60deg off the aircraft's velocity vector. Should the aircraft's subsequent flight path bring the area being viewed to within 15deg of the aircraft centreline, the radar automatically switches to the normal ground-mapping mode. Doppler beam sharpening is likely to be much used when projected specialized off-boresight guided weapons finally enter service.

Development of an effective pulse-Doppler radar of such small size was a formidable technical undertaking, so it was hardly surprising that several problems were experienced during early tests, particularly in look-down mode. Pulse-Doppler radars measure the Doppler shift created by target velocity in order to discriminate between genuine

Designate/
Return to
search

Weapon
release

Trim

NWS
A/R DISC
MSL STEP

Camera/
gun trigger

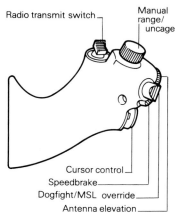

Radio transmit switch

Manual
range/
uncage

Cursor control
Speedbrake
Dogfight/MSL override
Antenna elevation

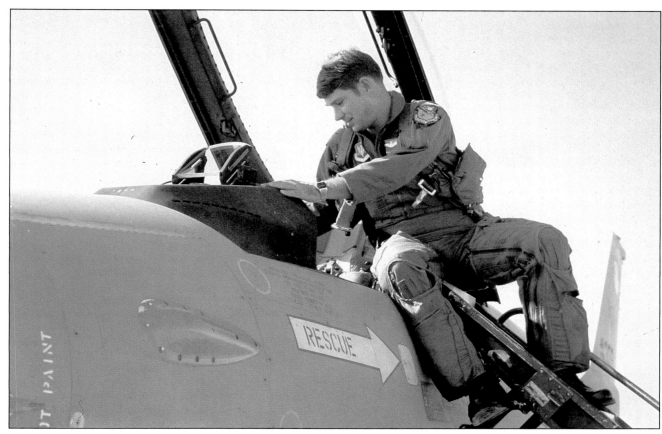

**Above: If the one-piece canopy were to fail, the combiner glass of the HUD would act as a windshield.**

targets and ground clutter. This involves defining a threshold velocity – a speed at which targets must be moving in order to be accepted as valid. Vehicles on West German autobahns often move at speeds of 100mph (160km/h) or more, and were sometimes registered as low-level targets.

During tests over water in Norway, false targets registered on the radar were found to be due to stray radiation from the radar antenna. In designing an antenna, the engineer would like to see all of the signal being directed into the main beam, but in practice some always escapes in the form of sidelobes – unwanted weak beams at an angle to the main beam. A good design will reduce these sidelobes as much as possible, but it is virtually impossible to eliminate them. Radar energy escaping from these sidelobes was being reflected off the water in fjords, creating false targets.

### Synthetic imagery
Earlier radars presented a direct radar picture to the operator, who could to some degree use his own skill and experience in deciding which targets were real. Sets such as the APG-66 reduce all radar data to digital form, and present the pilot with a synthetically generated image made up of pre-defined symbols. The screen is free from clutter and is much easier to read than that of earlier types of radar which showed 'raw' data, but the discrimination between real and false targets must be achieved automatically by signal-processing equipment. In the case of the early APG-66 sets, this feature required modification.

During other early trials, the radar

showed poor detection range and low performance in the Doppler beam-sharpened air-to-ground modes. Clearing up these and other 'bugs' took much time and effort, but the situation was under control by the summer of 1979. Modifications were made to the low-power RF circuitry, digital signal processor and system software, and the revised equipment was under flight test and evaluation by the end of 1979.

Improvements to the APG-66 form part of the MSIP update programme. In 1980 Westinghouse was awarded a $25 million contract to begin development

of a programmable signal processor (PSP) and dual-mode transmitter for the APG-66. The latter would use low PRFs for air-to-ground work, and medium to high PRFs in air-to-air combat. These modifications were intended to match the performance of the AMRAAM missile, and to improve air-to-ground capability and ECCM performance. The set would also receive track-while-scan and raid-assessment modes. Both new sub-units were designed to occupy the same space as the equipment they replaced.

The design of TWTs able to operate

efficiently over a wide range of PRFs is difficult. Given low or even medium PRFs, the transmitting tube of a radar spends more time silent than transmitting. In engineering jargon, the 'duty cycle' of time 'off' to time 'on' is low. The tube thus has plenty of time to cool between individual pulses, so the designer can work the device hard while it is actually radiating, obtaining high levels of peak power.

**Above right: Primary air-to-air radar mode is Downlook, a medium-PRF search and track mode able to detect low-flying intruders. According to Westinghouse, the set has a low false-alarm rate of less than two per minute. The radar displays use computer-generated alphanumeric and other symbology, to present the pilot with clean imagery, while the effects of clutter and system noise are filtered out by signal processing. Earlier-generation radars presented 'raw' analogue radar imagery to the user, requiring skilled interpretation.**

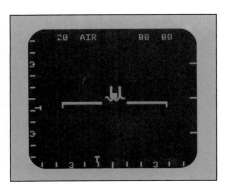

Range scale
Mode
Target altitude, 4,000ft MSL

Horizon line

Target symbol (track)

Target data block: Target's ground track
Target's calibrated airspeed
Aspect angle for intercept

Closure rate

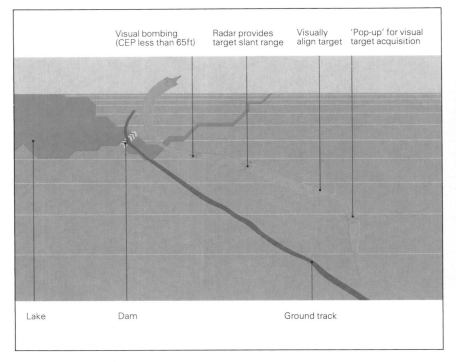

Visual bombing (CEP less than 65ft)    Radar provides target slant range    Visually align target    'Pop-up' for visual target acquisition

Lake    Dam    Ground track

Blind bombing (CEP less than 140ft)    Return to low level and follow head-up steering to target    'Pop-up' to get good radar picture of OAP then freeze – radar quiet    Dam    Low-level navigation

Bridge    Automatic weapon release    OAP is any point with known bearing and range from target    Lake    Ground track

**Above: During CCIP (continuously-computed impact point) attacks, the APG-66 radar is used to measure slant range to the target during the final run.**

At high PRFs, the tube spends much more of its time transmitting, and has less time to cool down between pulses, involving a duty cycle of 50 per cent or more. As a result, the amount of power which can be extracted in each individual pulse is reduced.

By the time that Westinghouse faced the problem of updating the APG-66, its great rival in the airborne radar business had developed a new type of TWT which made dual-mode operation much more efficient. Working in conjunction with Litton, Hughes had created a TWT able to cope with the high peak-power demands of low- and medium-PRF operation, while still operating efficiently at the high duty cycles required by high PRFs. Long-range detection performance at medium PRFs could now match that at high PRFs.

**All-round improvements**
The revised MSIP radar's high-PRF modes are expected to raise radar range by at least 30 per cent, and perhaps as much as 60 per cent. Track-while-scan facilities will match the set to the fire-and-forget multiple-target attacks made possible by the AMRAAM missile, while the extended range performance should allow maximum advan-

**Above right: CCRP (continuously-computed release point) attacks use the the ground mapping radar modes. A radar map may be created and 'frozen' during a pop-up manoeuvre.**

tage to be taken of the weapon's long range. The higher resolution of the modified set also allows the provision of a Raid-Assessment mode in which individual aircraft within a tight formation may be detected and tracked.

Improved air-to-ground facilities include new operating modes for ground target detection and tracking, plus Doppler beam-sharpening facilities for high-resolution ground mapping. These modes will complement the performance of the LANTIRN sensors.

Under the initial contract, seven radars were built for software development, ground trials and flight testing. Flight testing of the updated radar began in 1982. Earlier trials had involved the use of an F-4 testbed, but the new version was mounted in a modified Rockwell International Sabreliner business jet. The nose section of the aircraft was modified to carry the distinctive drooping profile F-16 radome. Delivery of revised radars should begin in 1984.

A second application for the APG-66 is the F-4EJ version of the Phantom. As part of a retrofit programme intended to extend the service life of the Japan Air Self-Defense Force fleet of Mitsubishi-built Phantoms, the existing APQ-120 radar is to be replaced by the APG-66J

derivative of the Fighting Falcon set. A total of 100 aircraft are to be reworked.

Hardware from the APG-66 is also being used in the new Offensive Radar System due to be fitted in the nose of the Rockwell International B-1B bomber. This equipment will be used for tasks including low-altitude terrain-following and avoidance, high-resolution ground mapping and target detection/tracking.

Development potential of the APG-66 is by no means exhausted. Westinghouse engineers are already predicting that future versions might be able to establish the identity of a target by analyzing the radar return, and that new air-to-ground modes might include terrain-following and high-resolution surveillance using synthetic-aperture techniques.

**The LANTIRN programme**
In the late 1980s, the APG-66 will be backed up by the Martin Marietta LANTIRN (low-Altitude Navigation and Targeting Infra-Red for Night) system. This equipment will allow the pilot of a single-seat aircraft to fly sorties by day or night and in adverse weather. It can provide terrain-following radar and FLIR (forward-looking infra-red) imagery for navigation; automatically acquire, identify and categorize tank targets, passing target information to the aircraft's fire-control system so that Maverick missiles may be launched against several targets in a single pass; and can acquire and track fixed ground

targets using FLIR or visual techniques, then designate them for attack using a built-in laser.

The basic installation comprises two avionics pods containing the sensors for navigation and target acquisition/tracking respectively. Martin Marietta is prime contractor for both. On the F-16, the pods will be carried on hardpoints under the inlet. They can operate autonomously, so an aircraft could fly into action with only one should this meet the requirements of the mission. Although the programme was formally launched in 1980, it was suspended just over a year later, and reshaped to reduced the technical risks involved.

The navigation pod is 12in (30.5cm) in diameter, 78in (198cm) long and weighs about 430lb (195kg). Main subsystems are a Ku-band terrain-following radar, wide field-of-view FLIR, pod computer and the associated power supply. Sophisticated signal processing is used to give the radar a wide azimuth coverage, allowing high-rate turns at low level in order to avoid or confuse the defences. This should give greater survivability than earlier-generation equipments which simply issued pitch commands to the pilot. The latter may have allowed him to avoid the terrain ahead, but exposed the aircraft to ground fire during the 'pull up' manoeuvre.

FLIR field of view is 28deg in azimuth and 21deg in elevation. The resulting wide-angle imagery may be superimposed on the outside scene by means of the HUD. In darkness or bad weather the HUD provides an image of TV-like quality and sufficient width to allow the pilot to look in the direction of his turn in order to 'preview' the terrain.

**Targeting pod**
The larger targeting pod has a movable nose section containing a FLIR sensor, laser transmitter/receiver and a stabilization system able to compensate for aircraft movements and vibration. A fixed centre section houses the tracker electronics and signal-processing systems and the boresight correlator used to pass target data to the aircraft's air-to-ground weapons. Environmental control of these systems and the nose-section sensors is handled by equipment in the aft section of the pod.

Flight testing using dummy fairings began in September 1982. The simulated pods have the same weight and mass distribution as the actual equipment and were instrumented to allow measurements of flutter, vibration and loads to be carried out. Test flying with functional equipment was scheduled to

**LANTIRN navigation pod (right) and targeting pod (below)**

Environmental control unit
Environmental control unit
Nose section assembly
Access panel
Target recognizer
Power supply
Missile boresight correlator
Control computer
Laser synchronizer/range computer
Central electronics unit

Powersupply
Built-in test maintenance/environmental control unit controller
Navigation FLIR
Radar interface unit
Transmitter
Radar antenna
Access panel
Radome
Receiver exciter
Pressurization unit
Radar power supply

begin in the summer of 1983 using two F-16B and two A-10A trials aircraft. By the winter of 1984, LANTIRN equipment is scheduled to have completed tests under adverse operating conditions during combined development test and evaluation/initial operational test and evaluation trials in Europe.

In a typical LANTIRN attack, the aircraft will perform a 'pop-up' manoeuvre at the initial point. Scanning to either side of the flight path, the sensors pass IR imagery to the target-recognition systems. Once targets have been assessed, they will be shown to the pilot on his head-down display, while the HUD marks the first to be engaged. Using a second cockpit CRT display to show IR imagery from the Maverick missiles, the pilot will assign the first round to its target. As one round is launched, the system will automatically set up for the next, allowing up to six targets to be engaged during a single pass. LANTIRN can also handle laser-guided munitions. In this case, the system would illuminate the pre-selected target as the aircraft pulled up and released its weapon.

The most technologically risky part of LANTIRN is the Automatic Target Recognizer (ATR) sub-system. The USAF no longer plans to incorporate this equipment into LANTIRN from the start, but to add it under a later retrofit programme. Competitive designs are being developed by Hughes and Martin Marietta for evaluation in mid-1984, and the result of this trial will determine whether either is to be committed to full-scale development.

Central components of the LANTIRN cockpit display are the Marconi Avionics HUD, and two head-down multifunction CRT screens. The latter are able to display data from the radar and infra-red imagery from the LANTIRN sensors or the Maverick missile seeker head, plus the system-status displays required by the pilot.

### LANTIRN funding

LANTIRN costs have been criticized by the US GAO, which ordered the USAF to re-evaluate its need for the equipment. In practice, says the USAF, the cost over-run has been less than 10 per cent – much of the alleged cost increase was due not to cost growth but to a change in accounting methods. The latter came about when LANTIRN was reclassified from being a retrofit programme of an existing weapon and upgraded to the status of being a programme in its own right. When this was done, the costs of development, testing and support became chargeable to the project and not to the F-16 programme. Further funding was added to allow for extra testing, and the programme has been stretched in timescale by about two years. To ease development, the USAF has dropped its requirement for LANTIRN to embody automatic laser correlation.

Flight trials of the LANTIRN HUD began in the summer of 1982, a year or so ahead of flight tests of the complete navigation and targeting pods. Congressional support for the project was waning, largely due to the high cost of the system, and the House Armed Services Committee reported that it had seriously considered 'recommending denial of all 1983 authorization of funding'.

Ford Aerospace has developed a FLIR pod for the US Navy, which will use it on the F/A-18 Hornet, and Congress has directed that this be tested in competition with LANTIRN before a production decision on the latter is taken in 1985. The USAF has in the meantime been prohibited from order-

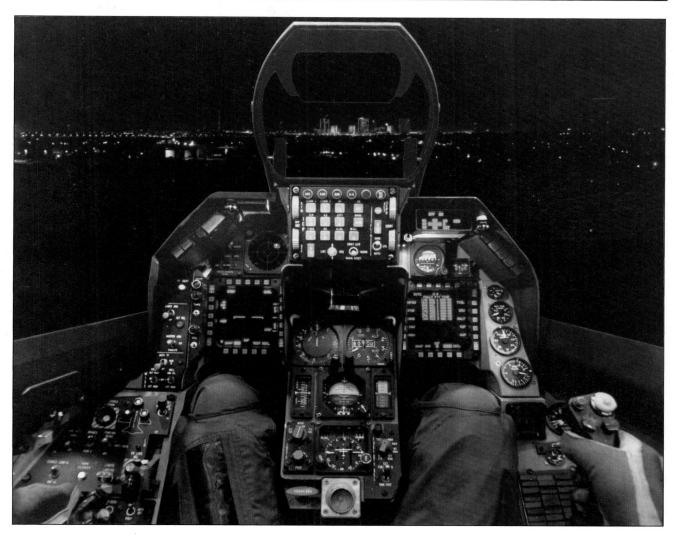

ing LANTIRN into production until competitive flight tests have been carried out.

### Cockpit displays

Data from the radar and Nav/attack systems of the Fighting Falcon are presented to the pilot on head-up and head-down displays. In the F-16A and B the head-down CRT display is manufactured by Kaiser, but for the HUD the USAF turned to the British company Marconi Avionics. A specialist in HUD technology, this Rochester-based company created the first HUD to enter service on a production aircraft – the Hawker Siddeley Buccaneer – back in 1960, and subsequently became an established supplier of HUDs to the USAF, building units for the A-7 Corsair II.

The original Buccaneer unit was primitive by modern standards, using analogue electronics and simple symbology. The A-7 HUD used digital electronics for computing and the positioning of the symbology, establishing the style of HUD now produced by many companies around the world. More than 2,000 units have been delivered for the Corsair II, and one of the company's HUDs was removed from the wreckage of an A-7 shot down in Vietnam, returned to the UK and found to be still in working order.

In addition to supplying the USAF, Marconi Avionics also provides equipment for other advanced military aircraft such as the Panavia Tornado, and had even developed the HUD for the Mirage F1.E contender for the NATO fighter order. For the Fighting Falcon programme, the UK company was involved from the beginning, having been awarded a contract to develop HUDs for the original two YF-16 prototypes. All subsequent patterns of HUD flown on or planned for the F-16 were designed by the same team.

In developing the F-16 HUD, the company placed great emphasis on the air-to-air gunnery role, aiming to create a system capable of giving a good first-burst hit probability. Radar ranging

would normally be used, but a rotary switch on the HUD front panel provides for the more traditional stadiametric ranging, using the known wing span of the target as a reference from which to compute range.

Since the entire canopy of the F-16 is a one-piece polycarbonate component, its loss in an accident or in preparation for ejection would expose the pilot to the full force of the slipstream. Design of the optical components of the HUD was contracted to the UK company Pilkington PPE, whose designers ensured that the combiner glass of the unit was strong enough to withstand the slipstream. With the canopy gone, the HUD can thus act as a temporary windshield.

Field of view of the F-16A/B HUD is 13·5deg in azimuth by 9deg in elevation. For the AFTI project a wider field of view was required, so the Rochester design team pushed conventional optical technology to its limits to produce an impressive 20 × 15deg field. For use

**Above: A wide-angle HUD and two multipurpose CRT head-down displays are the main new features of the F-16C/D cockpit. The HUD was originally intended to be a holographic unit.**

with the LANTIRN pod, the USAF asked for a HUD with an even larger field – 30 × 20deg. This forced the design team to return to the first principles of optics and devise an entirely new type of display.

The constraints on the HUD designer include the need to interfere as little as possible with the pilot's field of view, to take up as little of the instrument panel as possible, and not to intrude beyond the confines set by the windscreen and the ejection line. The last boundary is set by the space needed by the pilot's legs and feet during ejection.

To maximize the field of view the designer could mount the combiner glass as close to the ejection line as

**Above: Like the LANTIRN system itself, the Marconi Avionics holographic HUD is not certain to find a place in future F-16s. The USAF may modify the more conventional F-16C HUD to accept imagery from LANTIRN or other EO systems.**

**Above: Standard Marconi Avionics head-up display in an F-16A. The rectangular display seen below and to the left of the HUD control panel is not a radar display but forms part of the Fighting Falcon's sophisticated stores-management system.**

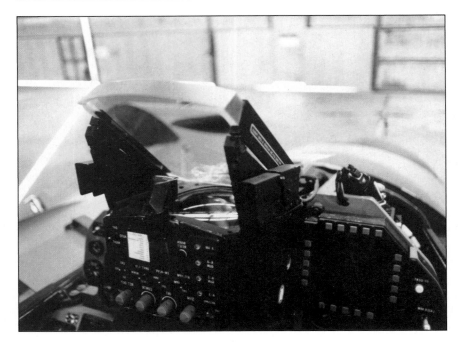

**Above: The wide-angle HUD devised for the AFTI/F-16 forms the basis of the F-16C HUD. This design offers the widest field of view possible using conventional optics.**

possible. This leaves no room for the traditional pattern of CRT image-injection system, since the latter is mounted on the pilot's side of the combiner glass and would thus project over the ejection line. A complex optical path involving 'folding' the light rays was devised, but this had a low efficiency, resulting in a dim view of both the CRT-generated imagery and the outside world.

The final solution entailed the use of a combiner consisting of a reflective hologram or diffraction grating to create the effect of a mirror surface. Holograms reflect light of only a certain colour, allowing light of all other colours to pass freely. In the LANTIRN HUD design, the colour chosen for reflection is the green associated with the CRT used to generate symbology. The combiner can thus act simultaneously as an efficient mirror and as a transparency. To quote Robin Sleight, Technical Manager of the Marconi Airborne Displays division, "We have found one of the rare conditions in life where we are getting something for nothing: a surface which transmits 90 per cent of the light hitting it, yet apparently also reflects to a similar value!"

The first unit was handed over to the USAF in March 1982, and flight tests aboard an F-16 started the same summer. Like the LANTIRN system itself, the holographic HUD faces an uncertain future. Early in 1983 Marconi Avionics announced that it had been awarded a contract to build a new pattern of HUD for the F-16C and D, but this is largely based on the AFTI unit rather than on the holographic design. It seems likely that the new unit will be modified for use with LANTIRN.

Under the MSIP programme, the F-16 will also receive new patterns of headdown cockpit displays. General Dynamics will install a moving-map display on an instrument panel between the pilot's knees, displacing conventional mechanical standby flight instruments. This system was chosen in preference to the synthetic raster-scan display favoured by GD, which would have allowed moving-map data to be displayed on any of three multi-function cockpit CRT displays being developed by Sperry.

## ECM systems

In addition to its offensive avionics, the Fighting Falcon is equipped with defensive electronic countermeasures (ECM) systems intended to help it survive in the face of modern air defences. Secrecy is essential if ECM techniques and tactics are to remain effective, so very little detailed information has been published concerning the performance of the equipment mentioned below.

The most basic item of ECM equipment is the radar-warning receiver (RWR). This is designed to detect the signals from hostile radars, and to alert the pilot that he is under observation. Most patterns of RWR give an approximate indication of the threat bearing, frequency and signal characteristics, while some identify the threat using a built-in catalogue of threat parameters.

When a threat radar is first detected by the RWR, the threat may not yet have detected the incoming aircraft. The RWR has the relatively simple task of detecting the powerful signal transmitted by the hostile radar, but the receiving system of the latter must attempt to detect the small amount of energy reflected by the target.

The threat radar will almost certainly be fitted with a relatively large and highly-directional antenna, while the RWR has only a low-gain omni-directional antenna array, but despite this inequality the RWR will usually detect the radar before the latter has detected the aircraft. Given this warning, the pilot may change course to avoid the radar, reduce cruise height in order to fly beneath the radar's horizon, or turn on some form of ECM. The warning provided by the RWR gives him a clear advantage.

The same techniques may be used if a tracking radar manages to lock on to the aircraft. The RWR display will probably give the first indication to the pilot that his tactics have been successful in 'breaking the lock' of the hostile system.

Basic RWR carried by the F-16 is the Itek ALR-69. Based on the earlier ALR-46, this was developed for the USAF and US Navy and consists of five general-purpose surveillance receivers plus a sixth frequency-selective receiver. The latter is probably used to detect signals associated with semi-active homing missile systems such as the Soviet SA-6 Gainful, and gives an indication of the direction of attack.

The US desire to limit exports of this sensitive equipment led to Pakistan rejecting its first batch of F-16s in 1982. These were to have been fitted with the Itek ALR-46. Widely exported to nations such as Egypt, Iran, Portugal, Saudi Arabia, South Korea, Switzerland, Taiwan, Thailand and West Germany, the ALR-46 covers the radar spectrum from 2.0 to 18GHz. Alarm indications are given on CRT cockpit displays and in the pilot's headset. Pakistan was eventually cleared to receive the ALR-69, but the older equipment may still be supplied to F-16 operators who do not face the most sophisticated threat systems.

At a later date, USAF aircraft could receive the latest RWR currently under development, the Itek ALR-74. This uses some of the technology developed for the US Navy's ALR-69, and is intended to counter Soviet threats anticipated for the late 1980s. Both programmes have attracted criticism from the US GAO, which wants to see a common RWR developed for both services.

Many F-16 operators have already opted to fit their aircraft with further ECM protection in the form of active jamming systems or chaff dispensers. The equipment selected is often specific to the individual air arm, although a degree of standardization is being attempted.

Modern jamming systems operate in noise and deception modes. Noise jamming aims to swamp the hostile radar signal or communications link with unwanted radio-frequency noise, so that the genuine and wanted signal cannot be distinguished from the background.

The technique is simple to implement, since very little needs to be known about the characteristics of the threats. If the exact operating frequency of the latter is known, the jammer may be pre-tuned to concentrate its output power on these frequencies. This is known as spot jamming.

If the threat frequency is not known exactly, or if the threat is frequency-agile, the simplest technique is to radiate the noise output of the jammer over a range of frequencies likely to contain the threat. This is known as barrage jamming, and is a simple technique, but the need to spread the power of the jammer reduces its effectiveness. Since the aircraft-mounted system can only generate a relatively modest level of jamming power, the signal-to-noise ratio received by the threat radar or system will be much lower than with spot jamming, easing the task of filtering out the wanted signal from the unwanted.

Rather than attempt such brute-force solutions, the modern jamming system uses a built-in search (or 'set-on') receiver to monitor the frequency of all detected threat signals. The output from this receiver may be used to control the frequency of the jammer transmitters, so that the spot jamming may be used against a threat of unknown or variable frequency.

## Deceptive jamming

More complex patterns of monitoring receiver may be used to allow subtler forms of jamming – a family of techniques known as deceptive jamming. These involve receiving the threat signal, processing it in some way, then re-transmitting it in the hope of persuading the threat system to accept the doctored signal as genuine. By choosing the manner in which the signal is processed before transmission, the ECM designer can feed false range or bearing information to an enemy radar, or even cause multiple false targets to be detected.

Demonstrating such false target jamming to the author several years ago, Westinghouse technicians effectively blanked out the circular PPI (plan-position indicator) display of a surveillance radar by generating thousands of false targets simultaneously. So closely were these spaced on the display that the CRT face literally turned an even shade of white.

In a modern jamming system the search receiver monitors all radar signals received, comparing their parameters with a built-in threat library. Once those representing the greatest threat to the aircraft have been identified, the jammer assigns the power available from its various jamming transmitters accordingly. This technique is known as power-management.

The type of jamming to be used will be chosen to match the threat, and the receiver will often monitor the hostile transmission at regular intervals in order to assess the effect of its jamming. If the latter is not proving effective, a different jamming method may be automatically selected.

In the early stages of the full-scale development programme, Tactical Air Command contemplated an internal ECM system. Studies of possible aircraft installations were carried out, and the likely balance between cost and aircraft survivability assessed. It was appreciated that an internal system would require the use of new technology and would take some time to develop and deploy.

All external stores had to be flutter tested, and some problem was initially experienced with the ALQ-119 ECM pod. When the aircraft was loaded with

**F-16 antenna locations**

VHF communications

Radar warning receiver

TACAN

APG-66 radar

Radar warning receivers

Radar warning receiver

TACAN

UHF communications/IFF

Glide slope/localizer

one specific configuration of stores, a speed limit had to be imposed. Tests with the ALQ-131 showed that carriage of the more modern pod required no such restraint.

Both the USAF and the Royal Netherlands Air Force adopted the ALQ-131 pod for the protection of their F-16 force. Selection of an ECM system for the F-16 became a major political issue in the Netherlands, with the Christian Democrat/Liberal coalition Government supporting the ALQ-131 and the Labour party being opposed to its adoption. The controversy was marked by Parliamentary hearings and debates. The US offer in August 1980 of a batch of 75 ALQ-131 ECM pods at a total cost of $63.5 million was the final factor which persuaded the RNethAF to adopt the standard USAF pod. This was seen as being cheaper than an internal ECM fit, and offered the advantages of standardization within NATO. Denmark and Norway were due to select an ECM fit in 1981, but lack of defense funds made it likely that no ECM would be fitted.

Development of the ALQ-131 started in the early 1970s to meet a USAF requirement. Following successful development and flight tests, the unit was ordered into production in 1976. ALQ-131 is a 573lb (260kg) modular pod-mounted system able to cope with a wide range of threats, particularly the radars and guidance systems of air-defence systems.

By selecting internal modules, the user may configure the pod to handle threats spread over one to five frequency bands. Modules are available to cope with all frequencies used by current anti-aircraft missile systems, and both noise and deception-jamming modes are available. The pod is power-managed, and the software can easily be modified to cope with the tactical situation which the user faces, or to take into account changes in threat tactics or parameters. Such modifications may be easily carried out, and may even be implemented on the flight line.

The struggle between the ECM designer and the latest tactics and systems is a continuous one. If the prospective enemy introduces new radar bands or techniques, hardware modifications may be needed. The USAF initiated the classified Have Exit update programme in 1980, four years after the equipment entered service. In this case, the system was probably being updated to cope with new Soviet threat systems featuring monopulse radars.

The USAF carries the ALQ-131 pod on the fuselage centreline hardpoint, thus losing the ability to carry an additional 300US gal (360Imp gal/1637l) of external fuel. It also left internal space available for follow-on systems such as AMRAAM-related equipment and the JTIDS (Joint Tactical Information Distribution System) data terminal.

**The Rapport III system**
After a study of the merits of pod-mounted and internal ECM systems, the Belgian Air Force decided in 1979 to adopt the Loral Rapport III (Rapid Alert Programmed Power Management of Radar Target) internal ECM suite. The original version of Rapport was developed for the FAéB following a study of the Mirage 5B carried out in the light of Israeli experience during the 1973 Middle East War.

Requests for proposals for an internal ECM installation were circulated to US and European electronics companies early in 1974. Three companies were contracted to carry out feasibility studies, a team consisting of Loral and MBLE being chosen to develop the prototype Rapport II. This was flight

**Above: If pod-mounted electronic countermeasures are carried on the F-16, the ventral hardpoint is normally used. This 388th TFW aircraft is equipped with a Westinghouse ALQ-119, almost certainly the (V)-12 version.**

**Right: Main recognition features of the Westinghouse ALQ-131 ECM pod are the full-length ventral gondola and two ventrally-mounted antennae. The red and black markings near the fore and aft-mounted radomes warn personnel to keep at least 15ft (4.6m) away when the pod is transmitting.**

tested in 1977 and entered production a year later.

Belgium demonstrated Rapport II to its NATO F-16 partners, but failed to arouse much interest. It then funded GD to carry out a study of a Rapport installation for the F-16. The GD response was favourable, so contracts for two prototypes of the Rapport III system for the F-16 were awarded to Loral and GD in 1979. Part of the system is carried in an extended fairing at the base of the tail fin. Rapport III is designed to be compatible with the Rapport II equipment still carried by Belgian Mirage 5R and 5BA fighters.

Before adopting Rapport the Belgian Air Force studied rival equipments, but concluded that the former system was likely to be cheaper than alternative US equipments. Being internally mounted, Rapport also has the advantage of not taking up a hardpoint and does not add to aircraft drag. One penalty which Belgium was forced to pay was the loss of internal avionics growth space, and the fact that the packaging of future avionics adopted by the NATO F-16 users would be non-standard on Belgian aircraft.

Flight trials of Rapport III were carried out during the summer of 1981 at Eglin AFB, Florida, using two Belgian Air Force F-16s. Units were flown against simulated threat systems and other equipment at the Eglin EW range.

The USAF did not carry out a full test of the equipment itself, but concluded from limited studies that the effectiveness of the ALQ-131 and Rapport III were broadly comparable. Minor technical problems delayed completion of the test programme, and while the equipment was shown to meet all requirements, the delays resulted in an

**Right: Aircraft cruising at medium altitude should be sitting ducks for hostile defences, but the ALQ-131 pod's noise and deception jammers can counter all known SAM systems.**

overrun in the trials budget.

This increased cost posed additional strains on what was already a tightly-funded programme, so Belgium was faced with the option of either voting additional funds or reducing the number of aircraft to be equipped from the planned 72. Not all Belgian F-16s will have Rapport, as the system will not be carried by aircraft assigned to the training role. Deliveries of hardware are due to end in 1985. The only other F-16 operator to adopt Rapport was the Israeli Air Force. The first Israeli order was for units to equip at least some of the 75 F-16s on order at that time.

According to Loral, Rapport is the first ECM system to integrate the tasks of detecting signals, identifying the threats and transmitting the required type of jamming signal. The system is reprogrammable on the ground in order to cope with new threat systems. Rapport systems for the Belgian Air Force are supplied by the Belgian company MBLE.

The wide-band RWR used in Rapport monitors all incoming radar signals, identifying the type of radar involved and displaying the resulting data to the pilot on a CRT. Power-management algorithms are used by the system's microprocessor-based jammer-control system in order to determine the best ECM tactics to cope with a constantly changing situation. Rapport employs forward and backward-facing jammers, whose output power and frequencies are set to match the characteristics of high-threat enemy equipments.

In 1979 the US Congress ordered the USAF and US Navy to evaluate Rapport III, but both declined to adopt the system. The USAF rejected Rapport III, pointing out that it was incompatible with the ALR-69 RWR, while the USN described the system as 'entirely unacceptable'. Both services were already collaborating on the inter-service Advanced Self-Protection Jammer (ASPJ) project.

Development of the ASPJ started as a competition between two industrial groups, with Westinghouse and ITT eventually defeating the Northrop/Sanders team. Space for ASPJ was always available within the F-16, but ECP350 introduced the necessary internal holes and ducts for the system's waveguides and wiring.

**Left: Lear-Siegler voice-control system from F-16/AFTI.**
**Below: Infra-red image obtained from the Oldelft Orpheus recce pod, to be used by RNethAF F-16s.**

**Above: The USAF has no current plans to deploy a dedicated reconnaissance version of the F-16, but the 6th full-scale development aircraft was flown with a dummy camera pod.**

So advanced is the design of the ALQ-165 ASPJ that the job was thought impossible by many people, according to Westinghouse. The Services were determined to obtain a system which would not suffer from early obsolescence as the threat systems it faced were updated. The designers decided to sever the pre-set relationship between threat and countermeasure which has been a feature of earlier ECM systems, and to rely on the ASPJ computer to select the appropriate countermeasure techniques in accordance with a combination of established threat data and real-time information obtained from the system's built-in receiver/signal processor.

The operational requirement called for ASPJ to cover several octaves of frequency, handling multiple threat signals against a dense background of other signals. The system can simultaneously jam many threats using its power-managed dual-mode transmitters. These have parallel TWT tubes which can be used to cope with pulse or CW signals in response to demands from the system software.

Design of the system is modular; the five basic sub-units plus the optional augmentation receiver and high-band transmitter may be installed aboard a range of aircraft. In the case of Fighting Falcon, the equipment is being mounted internally as part of MSIP Phase III. For the US Navy's F-14 Tomcat and F/A-18 Hornet, it will take up the internal space currently occupied by the ALQ-100/126 ECM equipment, while the US Marine Corps AV-8B will carry the system in an external pod.

**Communications equipment**

Basic communications installation in the F-16A and B consists of Collins ARC-186 VHF AM/FM and Magnavox ARC-164 UHF transceivers, a Magnavox KY-58 secure voice system and an interference blanker by Novatronics. Between 1984 and 1986 the USAF F-16 force will be equipped with the new JTIDS jam-resistant command, control and communications system, plus the Seek Talk ECM-resistant voice-communications equipment should this survive budget cut-backs.

Part of the MSIP Phase III programme, these units will be introduced at the same time as the LANTIRN electro-optical system, AMRAAM missile and the ASPJ electronic countermeasures system. Also introduced around this time will be new navigation equipment which will utilise the GPS satellite system. This will supplement the current Singer-Kearfott-developed SKN-2000 inertial navigation system.

One unusual item of communications equipment being pioneered in the AFTI/F-16 is a Lear-Siegler voice-control system. Designated Voice-Controlled Interactive Device (VCID), this is used to control the AFTI avionic systems. In its initial form the VCID system has a vocabulary of 32 words, but this will eventually expand to a maximum of 256. Early tests used words such as 'menu', 'data', 'entry', 'plus', 'minus', and 'recall', plus numbers, phonetic letters, and the points of the compass.

In the early stages of AFTI flight tests only single-word commands were used. These control nav/attack and flight-control modes, and later tests will evaluate the use of connected phrases. There are no plans at present to use voice command to handle critical safety-related functions such as primary flight control or weapon release.

In theory, electronic systems should be able to deal with complete sentences, searching for and extracting the relevant nouns and verbs. This type of parsing operation – a development of artificial intelligence research – can already be done via the keyboard of all but the smallest computers, and has been incorporated into computerized 'adventure' games such as Zork.

One problem with voice-recognition systems is that not only are they voice dependent – that is, they tend to respond accurately only to the voice for which they were set up – but that the accuracy also depends on voice characteristics remaining, if not constant, at least predictable. To explore this area GD conducted tests to see how voice quality changes owing to factors such as time of day, stress, fatigue, and G-loading. Other tests explored the effect on voice-operated systems of extraneous noise in the aircraft cockpit or in the pilot's oxygen mask, for example.

Noise level in the cockpit of a high-performance aircraft is very high; in the F-16 it can exceed 120dB during 9g manoeuvres. High g forces also make speech difficult or even impossible. During GD centrifuge tests, few pilots could talk at levels of more than 5g, although one individual managed to keep grunting commands at up to 9g. Under these rigorous circumstances, experimental voice-recognition equipment managed an impressive 90 per cent success rate in identifying his spoken commands. The USAF sees the major application of voice-operated cockpits as future night/all-weather single-seat fighters.

Another technique being tested in the AFTI/F-16 is a helmet-mounted sight for target designation. Instead of positioning target-identification cross-hairs by means of a throttle-mounted cursor control, the AFTI pilot need only look at a target in order to acquire it. The pilot aligns the target with a set of 0·5in (12·7mm) long cross-hairs incorporated in the visor of his helmet. He then depresses the 'target designate' button on his sidestick controller. Orientation of the helmet within the cockpit is measured by a magnetic system incorporating a transmitter mounted on the canopy immediately behind the pilot's head, and a 4oz (113gm) receiver system on the helmet; the radar or FLIR is automatically slewed to achieve lock-on. Final adjustment is carried out using the cursor controller or by voice command via the VCID system.

If the aircraft systems have detected a target, the location of the latter may be passed to the pilot via the helmet-mounted sight. In this case, miniature lamps at the tips of the visor cross-hairs indicate to the pilot the direction in which he must move his head to acquire the target. When all four are illuminated, the target is in the centre of the cross-hairs.

## Flight control system

Probably the boldest step in the original YF-16 design was the decision to adopt an all-electronic fly-by-wire (FBW) flight-control system, instead of the traditional pattern of hydromechanical system with linkages and cables. This was a high-authority command and stability-augmentation system of quadruplexed (four-channel) analogue type, and this configuration was retained for the production aircraft. The weight reductions resulting from the elimination of a mechanical system could be used to allow the large-scale use of fail-safe and fail-operative design techniques, ensuring the high reliability of the electronic equipment.

When details of the F-16 system were first published, they caused some misgivings at Saab-Scania in Sweden, where design of the JA-37 Viggen flight-control system was in hand, since the Swedes had opted for a quadruplexed digital system. Despite momentary misgivings, the Swedish decision was a correct one – Fighting Falcon was born too soon to embody a quadruplexed digital system. The latter first entered service in 1977 on the Space Shuttle and a year later on the F/A-18 Hornet.

Without the FBW system, the GD designers could not have positioned the aircraft centre of gravity behind the centre of pressure to give a reduced or negative static margin. The resulting inherent instability is controlled by the FBW system, making the aircraft easy to fly, but gives the controls a high response rate and allows the use of relatively modest amounts of tail deflection during high-g manoeuvres or supersonic flight. During the design of the YF-16, GD engineers estimated that the consequent reduction of trim drag allowed 400lb (181kg) to be shaved off the mission weight of the aircraft.

## Lifting tail

The use of relaxed stability also allowed the size of the tail to be reduced, as less force was needed to alter aircraft attitude. Since the tail effectively pushes the rear of the aircraft upwards in order to maintain level flight (the tail on a conventional aircraft pushes downwards), tail trimming forces increase the overall lift.

Adoption of FBW was a bold step, but one that paid off. The system has generally proved trouble-free in service, except for a brief period in August 1981 when most F-16 operators placed re-

This diagram illustrates an automated manoeuvring attack by the AFTI/F-16. During the initial run-in (1) the pilot engages the attack system, then carries out a pop-up

strictions on flying following the discovery of a problem in the flight-control emergency power system.

Ground test runs carried out following the loss of an F-16 in an earlier flying accident had focussed attention on an air-bleed valve. Following the crash of a 388th TFW aircraft on August 6, Time Compliance Technical Order 30 specified that this valve be inspected between flights until a modification was carried out. The check took 1–2 man-hours to perform, so most operators virtually grounded the aircraft until the valve had been modified to prevent 'chattering'.

Tests had shown that faulty valves could cause voltage fluctuations able to affect the flight control system's emergency backup systems, causing spurious and unpredictable pitch, yaw and roll inputs. Modifications to eliminate the problem took around 12 manhours per aircraft.

FBW systems have been test-flown since the late 1960s, and a rudimentary single-channel analogue system even flew as long ago as 1952 aboard a Tay-engined Viscount airliner testbed. The Panavia Tornado was the first production design to adopt FBW, but this aircraft retained a mechanical backup.

manoeuvre (2) to acquire the target and command lock-on. After a period of jinking flight (3) he updates the lock-on (4), then gives the system permission for weapon release (5).

The GD team was the first to take the step of eliminating mechanical backups, trusting the safety of the aircraft completely to electronics. Mechanical backups were also eliminated on the later F/A-18 Hornet, Mirage 2000 and JA-37 Viggen designs, but Fighting Falcon showed the way. For this reason alone, the GD warplane is assured of a place in aviation history.

For the AFTI/F-16, a full-authority triplex digital flight-control system is used. This is designed to be fault tolerant, so that no single fault should affect correct operation. In the event of a second fault developing, the system is able to revert to a standby condition which will permit safe flight to continue, allowing the aircraft to return to base in such an emergency.

Failures resulting in complete loss of control will be rare, the AFTI specification calling for not more than one per 10 million flight hours. To guard against unforeseen failure modes the system incorporates a simple analogue backup flight-control system. Designated the Independent Backup (IBU), this will allow control to be maintained should some drastic failure result in the digital flight-control system being unable to maintain control.

# Armament

**Ordnance carried by the Fighting Falcon ranges from simple weaponry such as unguided rockets and 20mm cannon shells to nuclear weapons. Air-to-air, air-to-ground and specialized anti-ship missiles, along with laser-guided 'smart' bombs, have all been cleared for service, and the F-16 is already slated to receive the most advanced types of weaponry currently under development, including the 'fire and forget' AMRAAM missile needed to cope with next-generation Soviet fighters. Even using straightforward 'iron' bombs, Fighting Falcon can hit its target with greater accuracy than the F-111.**

Despite its age, the General Electric 20mm M61A remains the standard USAF fighter cannon. The Service did attempt to develop a caseless 25mm weapon for the F-15 Eagle, but this project bogged down in technical difficulties, so the 20mm seems destined to soldier on through the 1980s.

The M61A1 may be a proven weapon, but its adoption in the F-16 resulted in some initial problems. Gun firing from the type was temporarily forbidden in September 1979 following two incidents in which this resulted in uncommanded yawing movements. Gun vibration was found to be affecting an accelerometer in the flight-control system, causing it to feed false data to the control computer, which in turn demanded the yaw.

A simple modification insulated the accelerometer from vibration. Ten aircraft were modified, assigned to Hill AFB, and successfully participated in a Red Flag exercise. The modification was then introduced into production aircraft, and all 106 operational F-16s delivered with the original pattern of accelerometer installation were modified during 1980.

In its F-16A/B form, the Fighting Falcon was armed with AIM-9 Sidewinder missiles for air-to-air combat. Today's Sidewinders are greatly improved versions of the primitive weapon which first entered production in the mid-1950s. Early Sidewinders may not have required the full cooperation of the target during air-to-air combat, but were restricted to use in classical tail-chase attacks in good weather.

With the arrival of second- and third-generation seeker heads, Sidewinder matured into an agile 'dogfight' missile. European F-16s were originally scheduled to carry the AIM-9J – a rebuilt and modernized version of the early AIM-9B or -9C – but the US Government eventually agreed to make the AIM-9L available. This is a highly agile weapon with all-new guidance seeker and proximity fuze. A total of at least 16,000 are likely to be built in the US, and a further 9,000 or more by a European manufacturing consortium.

## BVR missiles

In Vietnam, the MiG-17 and MiG-21 interceptors which challenged US warplanes were equipped only with cannon or short-range guided missiles. US pilots could opt to engage targets under beyond-visual-range (BVR) conditions using the Raytheon AIM-7 Sparrow, or close in to engage in a dogfight with guns and AIM-9 Sidewinders. By the time the F-16 was entering service in significant numbers, it faced the threat of aircraft such as the MiG-23 armed with AA-7 Apex long-range missiles. To engage these in a Sidewinder-armed F-16 would put the Soviet pilot in the same position as US aircrew had been in over Vietnam.

Without improvements, the Fighting Falcon stood the risk of becoming the late-1980s equivalent of the Japanese Zero – lightweight and agile but seriously under-armed. Romantics might argue otherwise, but the day of the simple fighter was coming to an end. Testifying before Congress in 1980, Undersecretary of Defense for Research and Engineering William J. Perry described the F-16A as "an incomplete airplane". Detailing the need for BVR combat capability, he said that "we kidded ourselves a little bit on the F-16, thinking we were buying an inexpensive airplane".

As originally planned, the APG-66 radar was not intended to have the capability of handling BVR missiles. What the customer asked for – and Westinghouse delivered – was a multimode set sized for the air-to-air mission but offering the many modes necessary for effective ground attack in the 1980s and beyond.

The definitive solution to the problem was the planned AMRAAM (Advanced Medium-Range Air-to-Air Missile), which was due to enter service in the mid-1980s, but USAF planners considered a number of interim solutions for service in the first half of the 1980s. French missile company Matra could offer a radar-guided version of the R.550 Magic. The US, meanwhile, had already fielded and withdrawn a radar-guided AIM-9C version of Sidewinder and had the technology available to develop an updated version of this as a result of the

**Above: 20mm cannon shells are loaded into the magazine of an F-16 at Kunsan Air Base, South Korea. A full load consists of 500 rounds.**

**Below: The smoke pouring from the F-16 on the target range comes not from the engine but from the 6,000rds/min M61A1 cannon.**

Semi-Active Medium Pulse-Repetition-Frequency Seeker Demonstration project carried out at China Lake. Either weapon would have given the F-16 a radar capability, but would have done little to improve the engagement range.

Obvious solutions were the longer-range AIM-7 Sparrow or British Aerospace Sky Flash radar-guided missiles. Although larger than AMRAAM, both missiles could provide the required range but would require modifications to the APG-66 in order to provide target-illumination facilities.

Evaluation of a Sparrow-armed YF-16 was carried out by GD, using company funding, with inert rounds carried on wingtip, underwing and fuselage-mounted pylons. The last location involved the pylon being fitted directly on the undercarriage door, and was used for test firings in November 1977. A test firing of the British Sky Flash missile followed a year later, using pylons in the same location.

The need for interim BVR missiles was questioned by some analysts, who claimed that the problems of target-identification would often inhibit BVR attacks, while the higher cost of the missiles would reduce the amount of live-firing training which would be possible. Adoption of either weapon would have been expensive, and AMRAAM development showed no signs of significant slippage in time-scale, so plans for the older missiles were shelved.

## AMRAAM and ASRAAM

Fighting Falcon will be the first aircraft to carry the new Hughes AIM-120 AMRAAM. This missile is intended to combine the performance of the AIM-7 Sparrow in an airframe not much larger than that of the AIM-9 Sidewinder. The weapon weighs only 326lb (148kg) at launch, compared with 115–195lb (70–88.5kg) for Sidewinder and 503lb (228kg) for the latest versions of Sparrow. Maximum range is more than 30 miles (48km), and the missile is likely to fly at around Mach 4.

AMRAAM flies the initial portion of its trajectory under the control of a mid-course inertial guidance unit which can be updated if neccessary by the launch aircraft. In the later stages of flight, the missile switches on its high-PRF radar seeker and homes onto the target. Since this seeker uses active radar, it does not require the launch aircraft to carry a target illuminator antenna or to continue to track the target after launch. If the target attempts to protect itself with jamming, AMRAAM's seeker can be set to operate in a medium-PRF home-on-jam mode during the midcourse or terminal stages of flight.

Hughes and Raytheon developed rival AMRAAM designs in the late 1970s. Each contractor was due to fire ten prototype rounds from F-14, F-15

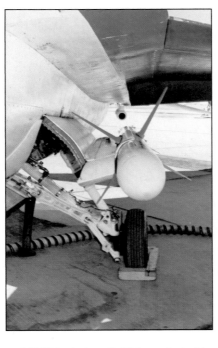

**Below: This unconventional door-mounted pylon was used for test firings of the Sky Flash shown here, as well as for Sparrow. No F-16 user has ordered the BAe weapon.**

**Below: the AIM-9 Sidewinder may be a lightweight missile, but lifting its 172lb (78kg) weight into place on the wingtip launch pylon requires significant muscle power.**

**Above: As a private venture, GD has test-fired radar-guided AIM-7 Sparrow missiles from the YF-16, though no customer has requested Sparrow armament.**

and F-16 test aircraft. Firings started in 1981, but after only six shots Hughes was declared the winner in December of that year.

The company launched its first test round in February, with the first guided shot (from an F-16) following on August 26. The round scored an almost central hit on a QF-102 target, which burst into flames and crashed. The missile did not carry a warhead. In a series of six design-validation flight tests, AMRAAM scored two direct hits, one near-miss well within the lethal radius of the warhead, and three failures. The design has now been modified to take account of the experience gained. Test firings will resume in 1984.

Under a $420-million 50-month contract awarded after the 'shoot-off', Hughes is to build some 100 development missiles, 87 of which will be

launched from F-14, F-15, F-16 and F/A-18 aircraft during a two-year series of development and operational test/evaluation firings. Delivery of production rounds will begin in the second half of 1985.

AMRAAM was nowhere near ready for service when the Multinational Staged Improvement Plan (MSIP) was approved in February 1981, but the associated Engineering Change Proposal ECP350 included changes to the aircraft structure and wiring of the wings to allow the weapon to be retrofitted easily at a later date.

The aircraft may eventually carry the shorter-range ASRAAM (Advanced Short-Range Air-to-Air Missile) being developed by a European consortium consisting of British Aerospace Dynamics and Bodenseewerk Geratetechnik. This missile is intended for US and

NATO use and would be built under licence in the USA. Development has been painfully slow, and any resulting weapon is unlikely to see service until the late 1980s.

In studying possible guidance systems for ASRAAM, the two companies looked at infra-red, active-laser and active-radar systems. One possibility would have involved using a combination of methods, some rounds with radar seekers supplementing others with IR heads in order to lessen the chances of enemy countermeasures proving successful. Marconi Space and Defence Systems proposed an active-radar seeker with a three-axis gimballed antenna able to provide the acute look-angles needed to acquire off-boresight targets.

Vectored thrust seems the most likely control system, since it would allow the

**Far left: Location of the M61A1 cannon, ammunition drum and feed in the F-16. GD studies have shown that 30mm DEFA, 27mm Mauser or 30mm Oerlikon KCA could be accommodated should a heavier and more destructive projectile be desired. Left: In creating the M61 series of aircraft cannon, the Armament division of General Electric revived the rotary principle first devised by the legendary Dr Gatling. This involves rotating the entire barrel assembly: while one barrel is firing, the remaining five are at different stages of the loading/unloading cycle. The result is a very high rate of fire and high reliability.**

high initial manoeuvrability needed to engage off-boresight targets. By eliminating wings, the design would allow three missiles to be carried on a single pylon.

## AGM-65 Maverick

The six underwing pylons and single under-fuselage hardpoint of the F-16 allow a heavy ordnance load to be carried, including air-to-surface missiles, 'smart' bombs, tactical nuclear weapons and conventional iron bombs. One of the most important warloads of US F-16s will be the Hughes AGM-65 Maverick used for precision attacks against point targets. This is available in AGM-65A, AGM-65B and AGM-65D forms, which use TV guidance, scene-magnification TV guidance and imaging infra-red (IIR) guidance respectively. The last can be used in day, night or adverse-weather conditions. Currently under development are the AGM-65E laser-guided version and AGM-65F IR-guided variants, but these are intended for use by the US Marine Corps and Navy respectively. All versions use common aft and centre sections and have the same aerodynamic configuration.

More than 26,000 TV-guided rounds were built, demonstrating an 86 per cent hit rate in 1,221 firings. Average miss distance during a series of tests against tank-sized targets was only 3ft (0.91m). A vidicon (TV) seeker in the nose of the missile may be slewed upon its two-axis mounting and used to view the target area. Using a TV image on the cockpit display, the pilot can align the target on the aiming mark, then command lock-on.

AGM-65A has a 5deg field of view, while the AGM-65B Scene Magnification variant has a 2.5deg field of view but can detect targets at longer range thanks to the increased image scale. These early-model Mavericks are not ideally suited to use from single-seat fighters due to the time needed to acquire the target and lock-on the missile seeker. Moreover, visibility conditions in many parts of the world can reduce target detection range to the point where the pilot of a high-speed aircraft no longer has time to operate the weapon. This problem has been appreciated for some time, spurring development of the IR-guided AGM-65D.

## Imaging infra-red

The operating principle of the IR version is similar to that of the -65A and -65B, but in this case a thermal image is displayed in the cockpit instead of TV. Two magnifications are provided – wide angle for target acquisition, and narrow angle for final identification and lock-on. One difference is that Maverick operations normally involve using the missile seeker to locate the target: with the IIR version, the seeker may be slaved to or cued by target-acquisition systems such as Pave Penny or LANTIRN.

**Above: After launching the fire-and-forget AMRAAM missile, the F-16 pilot will be able to turn away. The round will home onto the target during the final stages of flight using an active-radar seeker. Right: Internal arrangement of AMRAAM.**

After launch, the round flies a proportional-navigation course, cruising under the impulse given by a solid-propellant rocket motor. All versions of Maverick have roughly the same launch zone. The missile can be launched at dive angles of up to 60deg, while maximum launch altitude varies according to aircraft speed, and generally lies between 33,000 and 40,000ft (10,000–12,000m). Above this height the round would become aerodynamically unstable.

Maximum range varies according to aircraft speed and height – from more than 22nm (25 miles/41km) at Mach 1.2/40,000ft down to around 7nm (8 miles/13km) at Mach 0.5 at low level. At lower altitudes, maximum range is dictated by the loss of kinetic energy during the coasting stage of flight. Above 10,000ft (3,000m) or so, endurance of the thermal batteries used to provide on-board electrical power is the limiting factor. There is no minimum launch altitude, but the minimum launch range is constrained by the limitations of the guidance and the need for the launch aircraft to avoid the exploding warhead.

**Right: Destruction of a QF-102 drone by the first guided AMRAAM launch.**

**Below right: Internal arrangement of the TV-guided Maverick.**

**Below: Maximum range and height of Maverick launching have been declassified following the export.**

The first full-scale development F-16B releases a Maverick in a diving attack. An operational launch at such altitudes would require massive ECM protection for the aircraft.

The warhead is a 125lb (57kg) shaped charge unit with good secondary blast effects, and is effective against a wide range of tactical targets including moving or stationary armoured vehicles and trucks; artillery; SAM systems and their associated radars; and aircraft parked in revetments or hardened shelters. The warhead is located aft of the seeker, but the latter incorporates a 'tunnel' to allow the gas jet from the charge to pass freely. (An alternative penetrator/blast-fragment warhead developed for the USN and USMC versions is fitted with selectable fuzing so that it can be set to detonate either on initial impact with the target, or after penetration.)

Maverick requires little modification of the parent aircraft, and can be carried on the three-round LAU-88/A and LAU-88A/A launchers or the single-rail LAU-117/A. A modified version of the LAU-88/A with drag-reducing fairings, including a 'boat-tail' aft section, is in-

**Above: The weapon which Fighting Falcon may never see – funding for the Hughes Wasp mini-missile was effectively cancelled in 1983.**

**Above: 1,000lb (454kg) iron bombs are released from the first F-16XL.**

**Top right: Two-seat F-16/79 launches a Paveway laser-guided bomb.**

tended for use on high-performance aircraft such as the F-16. Drag is reduced by some 45–60 per cent depending on flight profile. Mavericks can be loaded on to the launcher and go/no-go tested as a complete assembly.

Modifications to the LAU-88/A have been devised to allow rapid fire against multiple targets. The modified launcher contains facilities for: ground boresighting all missiles to the 'pipper' of the aircraft sighting system; operating two missiles at the same time, with the seeker head of the second slaved to that of the first; holding the aim of the second round after the launch of the first; and providing a safe time interval between dome cover ejection and missile launch.

One Maverick tactic tested during AGM-65D trials during 1982 involved the use of an F-16 and an F-111 working as a 'hunter-killer' team. Using a belly-mounted AVQ-26 Pave Tack FLIR pod, an F-111F was able to locate and designate a ground target, then use a voice link to call in the Maverick-armed F-16.

An important future weapon for the F-16 might be the Hughes Wasp mini-missile. Intended to be a relatively inexpensive and lightweight (approximately 105lb [48kg]) weapon, Wasp will be launched in multi-shot 'fire-and-forget' attacks. Most tactical guided missiles must be locked on to their target before launch, but the advanced-technology millimetre-wave (94GHz) active radar seeker fitted to Wasp will be able to search for, locate and identify tactical targets after being launched, and without assistance from the launch aircraft. Wasps will be fired from 12-round launch pods, two of which would be carried by an F-16. Flight tests began in November 1982.

**Above: The F-16/79 releases iron bombs over a US range. European air arms have long since abandoned medium altitude dive attacks, but the USAF has great faith in ECM.**

In August 1978 one of the YF-16s became the first single-seat aircraft to deliver smart bombs without assistance from a second target-designating aircraft during a series of 46 industry-sponsored test flights carried out in 1978. For these tests, the aircraft carried a Martin Marietta/Thomson-CSF Atlis pod under the intake.

Developed by Martin Marietta and the French company Thomson-CSF, Atlis (Automatic-Tracking Laser Illumination System) is a pod-mounted system consisting of a stabilized TV system able to lock on to targets selected by the pilot, and a target-designation laser able to 'mark' targets during missile or smart bomb attacks. It allows the aircraft to break away immediately after missile launch in order to avoid being engaged by enemy point-defence systems. During the first trial, the aircraft delivered a GBU-10 bomb from an altitude of 5,000ft (1,524m), entering a 4g turn immediately after weapon release.

**Simulated Sabre trials**

As part of the same series of tests, the YF-16 carried out a series of simulated attacks to prove the concept of the planned British Aerospace Sabre air-to-ground missile. Based on the well-proven Rapier anti-aircraft missile, Sabre was intended to allow Royal Air Force pilots to engage several off-boresight ground targets during a single pass.

There was no significance in the use of the YF-16 for these tests – BAe engineers needed a trials aircraft fitted with modern avionics and HUD, and took advantage of the US programme. The test flights at Edwards AFB followed a series of tests in the Martin

**Right: 388th TFW Fighting Falcons set course on a training mission.**

**Below right: Penguin anti-ship missile under the wing of an RNoAF F-16.**

Marietta combat simulator, and thousands of mathematically modelled 'firings'.

The results of these tests showed that the number of targets engageable in a single pass would be roughly equal to the range in kilometres of the distance at which the first was detected: some four seconds were needed to align the laser system on to the first target, and re-aiming on to a fresh target following the kill would take several seconds. A typical squadron pilot would manage a kill rate of around 70 per cent.

Development of Sabre cost £1.5 million of company funding, but the weapon was not adopted by the RAF. That service opted instead to fund development of the Hunting Engineering VJ291 guided cluster bomb, but the latter project was itself abandoned in the summer of 1981 owing to technical problems and escalating costs. Atlis was not adopted by the US services, but is due to equip some French Air Force Jaguars and Mirage 2000s.

Some F-16 operators will carry their own specialized weapons on the F-16. To guard against the possible effects of a future arms embargo, Israeli aircraft might be modified to carry the indigenously-developed Raphael Shafrir 2 heat-seeking missile or the follow-on Python 3. The former entered service in 1969 and is reported to have scored more than 200 'kills', with a single-shot kill probability of 60 per cent. Python was scheduled to enter service in 1983 or 1984, but pre-production rounds were given a baptism of fire during the 1982 air combats over Lebanon.

Norwegian Air Force F-16s will carry the Kongsberg Vapenfabrikk Penguin 3 anti-ship missile. Derived from the sur-

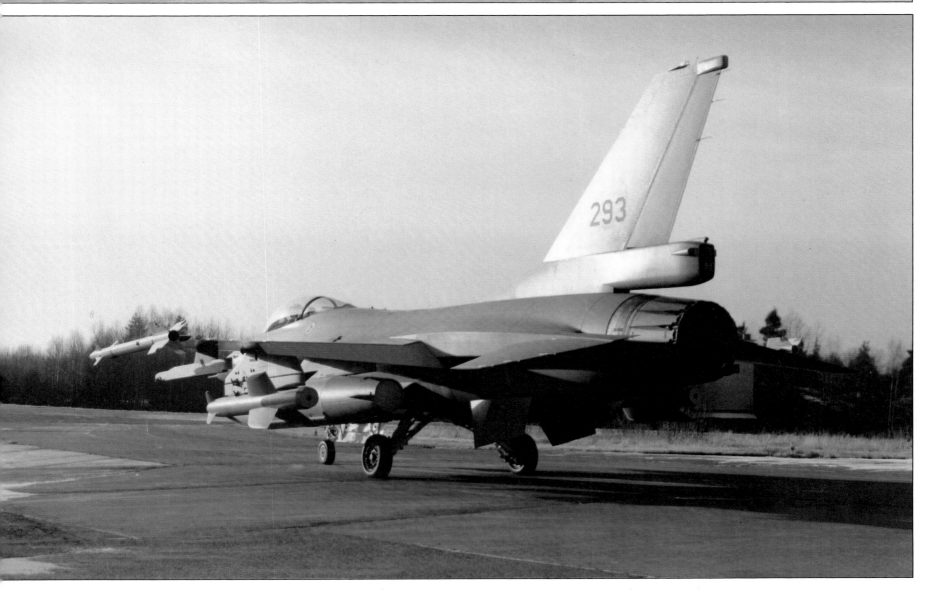

face-launched Penguin missile, this lacks the solid-fuel booster rocket of the standard missile and has smaller wings. It can carry a 250lb (113kg) high-explosive warhead over ranges of up to 25 miles (40km), depending on the speed and height of the aircraft at the moment of weapon release.

Warload of the arrow-winged F-16XL is much improved over that of the standard aircraft. A total of 29 hardpoints beneath the wings and fuselage can carry 15,000lb (6800kg) of stores, allowing a payload of 16 Mk82 bombs to be carried under the wings and on the centreline.

The F-16XL was the first aircraft to be designed for semi-conformal carriage of weaponry. If an aircraft carries a heavy load of external ordnance and stores on the conventional patterns of external pylon, the drag of such equipment may exceed that of the airframe, dramatically reducing range and speed while increasing radar cross-section. If conformal carriage is adopted, stores and weapons are designed to 'blend' into the airframe.

Such a technique offers dramatic reductions in drag, but taken to its extreme would involve stores being redesigned to match the shape of the parent aircraft. In practice, however, much of the promised advantage may be obtained by less drastic redesign efforts.

In 1970, the USAF and US Navy jointly funded a programme of conformal-stores trials, during which Boeing installed a large, shallow ventral pallet under the fuselage of an F-4B test aircraft. This could carry several configurations of stores, such as a load of 12 Mk82 500lb (227kg) bombs mounted in four rows across the width of the fuselage. Each row contained three bombs stowed nose-to-tail.

Flight trials showed that the modified aircraft had less drag than a clean F-4, the pallet having improved the area distribution of the Phantom design. Loaded with weaponry, it could fly in clean condition a mission which would normally demand the carriage of two 370US gal (308Imp gal/1,402 litre) external fuel tanks, while the maximum speed at around 30,000ft (9,000m) with a payload of up to 12 500lb (227kg) bombs rose from Mach 1.1 to Mach 1.8.

Despite such obvious success, the services did not retrofit their F-4 fleets. The modification would have cost no more than $75,000 per aircraft in 1971 prices, but the planning of the time was based on the erroneous assumption that the Phantom would be phased out by 1982.

## Range improvements

In the case of the F-16XL, stores are semi-buried in the airframe. Wind-tunnel tests carried out prior to the aircraft's first flight suggested that gains of up to 50 per cent in mission radius might be possible.

Positioning of the bombs on the XL follows the contours of the aircraft underside. On the inboard stations, the bomb nearest the front is carried slightly nose-up, those further back are virtually level, while the aft bomb is mounted nose down. Individual stores are distributed around the aircraft centre of gravity in order to eliminate destabilizing effects. According to GD, the positioning of bombs is staggered to create a drag-reducing effect similar to that produced by area ruling of the airframe cross-section.

Instead of using the traditional pattern of stores pylon and ejector units, the GD designers substituted a lightweight 30lb (13.6kg) ejector, shaving a total of 1,500lb (680kg) from the weight of the complete aircraft.

**USAF F-16 stores loadings:**
**1: AIM-9 Sidewinder. 2: AIM-7 Sparrow (proposed). 3: AIM-120 AMRAAM. 4: ALQ-131 ECM pods. 5: Electro-optical/infra-red/terrain-following radar pods. 6: Up to 25 Mk82 1,000lb (454kg) bombs. 7: Mk84**

**2,000lb (907kg) bombs. 8: and 9: Paveway or GBU-15 laser-guided bombs. 10: Up to 17 cluster bombs. 11: AGM-45 Maverick. 12: 370gal fuel tanks. 13: 300gal fuel tank. 14: 600gal fuel tanks.**

1 AIM-9L Sidewinder
2 AIM-9J Sidewinder
3 Durandal anti-runway weapon
4 AIM-120 AMRAAM
5 Wasp air-to-surface mini-missile (proposed)
6 Orpheus recce pod (RNethAF only)
7 Penguin Mk 3 anti-ship missile
8 Cluster munition
9 ALQ-131 ECM pod
10 Nuclear bomb
11 GEPOD 30mm gun pod
12 AGM-109 MRASM cruise missile (proposed)
13 SUU-25 flare
14 TV or IIR-guided AGM-45 Maverick
15 SUU-20 practice carrier
16 LAU rocket launcher
17/18 proposed electro-optical, FLIR and radar pods

19 ATLIS II designator pod (trials only)
20 Paveway laser-guided bomb
21 Mk 82 500lb (227kg) general-purpose bombs
22 HOBO 'smart' bomb
23 Mk 84 2,000lb (907kg) general-purpose bomb
24 Mk 82 Snakeye retarded bomb
25 External fuel tank
26 AGM-78 Standard ARM anti-radar missile
27 Mk 83 1,000lb (454kg) bomb
28 Mk 117 750lb (340kg) bomb
29 AGM-45A Shrike anti-radar missile
30 AGM-88 HARM anti-radar missile
31 Radar-detection pod (for proposed Wild Weasel two-seater)

**Left:** Even with simple iron bombs, the F-16 offers exceptionally accurate delivery. During some trials, diameter of the weapon impact area was only one third of the specified figure.

**Right:** During low-altitude attacks, the tail fins of the Snakeye 500lb (227kg) bomb open to retard the weapon. The impact point is thus well to the rear of the aircraft, protecting it from blast and debris.

**Above:** The impressive array of stores carried by, tested on or designed to be compatible with the Fighting Falcon belies the type's original conception as a cheap and simple lightweight fighter.

**Right:** USAF technicians check 500lb (227kg) bombs on a munition cart, prior to loading them aboard an F-16 during exercise Cope Elite 81. As a result of MSIP modifications, all hardpoints are likely to be cleared to a 9g load factor.

# Combat and Deployment

Ordered by the USAF, adopted by four NATO air arms and high on the shopping list of the Imperial Iranian Air Force, the F-16 was never far from the headlines in the late 1970s. With three production lines tooled up, aircraft were delivered in ever-increasing numbers, and other air forces joined the queue to take delivery of General Dynamics' latest creation: by mid-1983 Fighting Falcon had already been ordered by ten nations in five continents. And if Israel's 1967 air strikes were the best advertisement for the Mirage III, the Osirak raid may yet boost sales prospects for the F-16.

The USAF accepted its first production F-16 on August 17, 1978, and the first delivery to an operational unit followed on January 6, 1979. First unit to be equipped was the 388th Tactical Fighter Wing at Hill AFB, Utah, which built up to its full strength of 102 Fighting Falcons by the end of 1980, and trained aircrew for TAC and export customers.

In the hands of 388th TFW pilots, the Fighting Falcon began to show its mettle. Three days of war games held at Hill AFB in March 1980 showed how the aircraft could be used to reinforce the NATO Central Front or any other trou-

**Below: The long range of the Fighting Falcon allows staging flights from the US to Western Europe without assistance from European-based tankers. On trials, aircraft have flown 2,000nm without refuelling.**

ble spot. Refuelling from KC-135 tankers, 12 aircraft carried out a 7,000km (4,350-mile) transit flight lasting 10 hours to simulate overseas deployment, followed by two days of intensive flying.

Despite the sophistication of the new warplane and its avionic systems, the care taken during design and development to ensure reliability and easy maintenance paid off from the beginning, and unit after unit converting to the type found itself clocking up flying hours at a higher-than-predicted rate. In 1979 the average number of hardware failures per flight hour for USAF aircraft was around 1·2, against an eventual goal of only 0·34. During the second half of 1979 the actual failure rate of the F-16s at Hill AFB varied from just under 1·2 down to around 0·75, and this showed signs of falling to the target figure by the early 1980s.

By 1980 the F-16 was displaying impressive reliability in the field. Tactical Air Command standard for mission capability is 70 per cent, but by 1980 the Fighting Falcon was averaging 74 to 76 per cent, making it the most reliable fighter in the US inventory. Both figures quoted refer to the number of aircraft completely or partly mission capable.

A study carried out in 1976 identified many areas of F-16 operations which would be cheaper than those associated with the earlier F-4. This assumed a typical TAC squadron of 24 aircraft and identified the cost changes (in 1976 prices) detailed in the accompanying table. All other cost such as support equipment and base matériel support were assumed to be unchanged. On this basis the annual operating cost of an F-16 squadron would be 30 per cent less than an equivalent F-4 unit.

**Above: Infantrymen watch an F-16 take off during Exercise Team Spirit 82. Fighting Falcons have taken part in many recent exercises.**

Fighting Falcon officially started its operational career with the USAF on November 12, 1980, when the 4th Tactical Fighter Squadron – part of the 388th TFW – achieved Initial Operational Capability. In March of the following year this unit took 12 Fighting Falcons overseas for the first time during a month-long deployment to Flesland in Norway. If further proof were needed that the Fighting Falcon was a success, this was provided in June 1981 when seven 388th TFW aircraft won the Royal Air Force-sponsored tactical bombing competition held at Lossiemouth in Scotland, defeating RAF Jaguars and Buccaneers and USAF F-111Es.

Delivery of the 400th aircraft took place in May 1981, the 500th production example following in August of the same year. First USAF pilot to clock up 1,000 hours was Lt Col Dean Stickell of the 16th Tactical Fighter Training Squadron at Hill AFB. He reached four figures of Fighting Falcon flying time in the autumn of 1981, his involvement with the aircraft having begun at Edwards AFB during the type's development and evaluation programme.

### Increasing orders

By this time the USAF had 1,388 Fighting Falcons on order, and was talking of ordering a total of almost 1,750 examples for regular Air Force units, plus enough to re-equip the Thunderbirds display team. A possible order to re-equip Air National Guard units was seen as likely to add 600 to 800 further aircraft to the production run. Consideration was also given to storing 150 aircraft in Israel in kit form.

By the summer of 1981 overseas deployment of the Fighting Falcon had begun with the first deliveries to the 8th TFW. Part of the Pacific Air Forces and based at Kunsan in the Republic of Korea, the wing began converting from the F-4D in September 1981. Although a long way from the continental USA, the wing has maintained good operational readiness despite a shortage of spares – a common F-16 problem as more and more squadrons converted to the type. The majority of newly-built components were immediately embodied in new-production aircraft, rather than being shipped to the user as spares. Availability rates of 70–75 per cent were reported early in 1983, partly as a result of earlier Block 10 aircraft being swapped for the then up-to-date Block 15 standard. Basic mission of 8th TFW is strike and interdiction, but air-to-air combat training is also carried out. F-4s released from service at Kunsan were returned to the USA and re-assigned to Air Force Reserve units.

F-16s from USAF Korean bases act as 'friendly enemies' for F-15 units in Japan, allowing USAF aircrew assigned to the latter location to practise dissimilar air combat. During other exercises, techniques have been developed for operating the two types in a co-operative manner. Fighting Falcons can join an F-15 formation to take advantage of the latter's longer-ranged Hughes APG-63 radar and the attrition inflicted by the Eagle's AIM-7 Sparrow missiles in the opening stages of an air combat.

By the spring of 1982, the USAF fleet had exceeded 100,000 flying hours. A total of 345 was in service at that time,

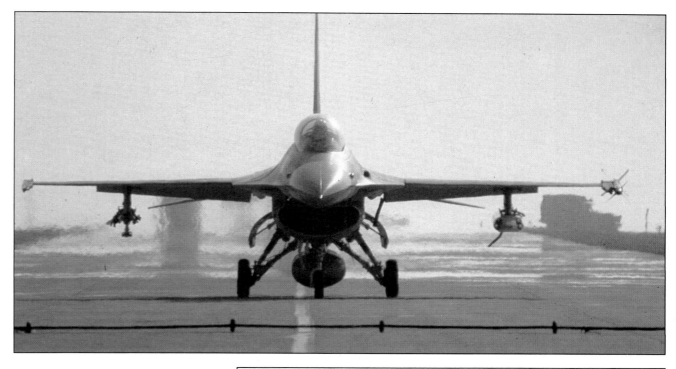

**Above: Fighting Falcons often carry a ventral tank, but runway clearance when this store is fitted is clearly minimal.**

### Comparative annual operating costs

(one TAC squadron of 24 aircraft, 1976$ × 1,000,000)

| Element | F-4 | F-16 |
|---|---|---|
| Fuel | 4·3 | 2·1 |
| Training | 1·1 | 0·3 |
| Munitions & missile training | 1·1 | 0·9 |
| Spares | 1·8 | 1·2 |
| Base operating support | 1·7 | 1·3 |
| Depot Maintenance | 2·9 | 2·3 |
| Safety/logistic modifications | 0·4 | 0·6 |
| Military pay & salaries | 7·5 | 5·4 |
| Medical facilities | 0·3 | 0·5 |

270 with TAC operational units. Deployment of the aircraft to USAFE in West Germany started in December 1982, and the 50th TFW became operational on the type at Hahn Air Base in July 1982.

The first unit to become operational at Hahn was the 313th TFS. Following initial training at Zaragoza in Spain, the unit took its 24 F-16s to Hahn in the spring of 1982. Later that year the 50th TFW and 496th TFS also began re-equipping to bring the Hahn wing up to strength. Aircraft assigned to Hahn were to Block 15 production standard. This includes the larger horizontal tail

**Below right: The 388th TFW was the first operational F-16 unit. During Exercise Yellow Alpha in 1980, 18 of its aircraft flew an impressive total of 72 'combat' sorties.**

surfaces, and inlet hardpoints for AMRAAM missiles and LANTIRN sensors.

One highly-publicized conversion to the Fighting Falcon was that of the USAF's Thunderbirds display team. The team made no public appearances in 1982 following a four-aircraft crash which killed four members of the group. At that time, the team was using T-38 Talon trainers, but eight F-16s were assigned to the unit in the autumn. Several paint schemes were evaluated before the definitive black/red/white finish was approved. The Thunderbirds completed the transition to the F-16 in November 1982, and were thus able to fly the new type during the 1983 display season.

Starting in October 1982, the US Air National Guard began to deploy the F-16. First ANG unit to re-equip was the

**Above: First USAFE Fighting Falcon unit was the 50th TFW at Hahn. Deployment started in December 1982 and was completed in 1983.**

169th Tactical Fighter Group at McEntire AFB, which received 24 Fighting Falcons in 1983 as replacements for its A-7 Corsairs. First AF Reserve unit to get the F-16 will be the 466th TFS at Hill AFB, Utah. Currently equipped with F-105 Thunderchiefs, this unit will re-equip with Fighting Falcons in 1984.

As aircraft continue to roll off the production lines, the USAF Fighting Falcon strength will continue to build up. In 1983, another F-16 wing, the 401st TFW, became operational at Torrejon in Spain. Next to become operational will be the 86th TFW at Ramstein AFB, West Germany.

**Below: The 'bubble' canopy of Fighting Falcon gives good visibility. Even at high angles of attack, the pilot has a clear view over the nose of his aircraft.**

**Above: It is rare to see Fighting Falcons in the clean condition of these KLu examples – even the wingtip rails are empty on the two nearest aircraft.**

**Left: Two decades of aerospace technology lie between the lumbering Tu-95 Bear and its KLu 'escort'. The Soviet aircraft may have been on a mission aimed at measuring the 'scramble' response time of the F-16.**

An additional F-16 wing made up of two squadrons – 50 aircraft in all – is scheduled for deployment at Misawa air base in northern Japan from 1985 onwards. This is intended to help offset the build-up of Soviet arms in the region. The deployment plans were attacked as 'provocative and hostile' by the Soviet Union when they were announced in the autumn of 1982.

The 1984 US defence budget allocates a total of $2,300 million to F-16 procurement in 1984, and $3,200 million in 1985. This will allow production to run at 120 aircraft per year. This may seem a long way from the original concept of a 'cheap' fighter, but if used to buy F-15 Eagles, the same money would enable only half that number to be procured.

### F-16 exports
In 1977 the US estimated the likely market for Western-built fighters over the next two decades as 6,000. Main candidates at that time were seen as the

US Grumman F-14 Tomcat, McDonnell Douglas F-15 Eagle, General Dynamics F-16 Fighting Falcon and McDonnell Douglas F-18 Hornet, the Anglo-German-Italian Panavia Tornado, and the Dassault-Breguet Mirage 2000 from France. This impressive line-up was joined within a few years by the General Dynamics F-16/79 and Northrop F-20 Tigershark from the US, and the Dassault-Breguet Mirage IIING, and the future may see further candidates in the shape of the Saab-Scania JAS 39 Gripen from Sweden, Israel Aircraft Industries' Lavi, the Dassault-Breguet ACX, and the planned tri-national Advanced Combat Aircraft (ACA).

The Fighting Falcon was to be a candidate for many export orders. The type's adoption in 1975 by the air forces of Belgium, Denmark, the Netherlands and Norway was a major boost, but the F-16 was soon to be locked in competition with its rivals in the search for overseas orders.

In the early stages of the programme, the USAF opposed early delivery commitments being made to nations outside the multi-national manufacturing consortium, except Iran. In order to avoid a shortage of aircraft and spares, the service did not want to see further export commitments until 1981. In practice, however, the Department of Defense and General Dynamics continued to promote the aircraft, but no early sales agreements were reached.

The Force Aérienne Belge/Belgische Luchtmarcht (Belgian Air Force) was the first European operator to take delivery of locally-built Fighting Falcons. The original Belgian order was for 116 aircraft – 96 single-seaters and 20 two-seat trainers – and the first example was accepted on January 29, 1979.

On January 16, 1981, 349 Sqn of the FAéB was officially assigned to NATO, and on May 6 it was declared fully operational. Belgium will deploy three F-16 wings. No 1 Wing at Beauvechain

consists of two squadrons – 349 and 350 – each with 32 aircraft. The latter squadron was the second FAéB unit to convert to the type. 10 Wing at Kleine-Brogel consists of 23 and 31 Squadrons. As F-16 conversion continued, the MTU was transferred from Beauvechain to Klein Brogel. Once conversion is completed it will disband, and key staff will move to the FAéB Technical School at Saffraanberg.

Within two years of taking delivery of its first F-16As the Belgian Air Force reported an availability rate of 88 per cent. Mean time between failures was 2·9 hours, while the 12 man-hours of maintenance required per flying hour was well below that of many earlier types. Turnaround time was between 15 and 45 minutes, depending on the type of mission being flown.

The Belgian Air Force was the first to use the Fighting Falcon in the somewhat unwarlike role of target tug. Tests carried out at Solenzara in Corsica using a No 1 Wing aircraft tested various underwing and fuselage locations for the pods associated with Tetraplan and Secapem B90 targets, as well as the newer Taxan design which incorporates an acoustic scoring system. These tests included jettison trials in which an Alpha Jet was used as photographic chase plane.

Belgium's F-16 force will be boosted by a further wing in the late 1980s when the Dassault-Breguet Mirage 5B is phased out of FAéB service. The Mirages currently serve with Nos 2 and 3 Wings, attrition having reduced the number operational to around 60. Starting in 1988, therefore, the service will replace the Mirage force with a follow-on batch of 44 F-16s due to be delivered in 1988/9. The deal is worth $625 million. Industrial offset arrangements offered by GD would be 58 per cent – the figure used in the original F-16 deal – plus a further 22 per cent going to Flemish companies in northern Belgium. When the new aircraft are operational, Belgium will field eight Fighting Falcon squadrons, or a total of 160 aircraft.

### Continuing production
Production of the F-16 in Belgium would have ended in 1984 once the 116 aircraft ordered under the original 1975 deal had been completed, but GD has offered to place enough offset work on USAF and export aircraft to keep the line moving until work starts on the next Belgian batch in 1987.

Beginning in September 1981, a total of 35 early-production Belgian Air Force F-16s were rotated back through the SABCA factory at Gosselies in Belgium for cockpit modifications and updating of the avionics, including the APG-66 radar. This work followed the completion of intensive operational evaluation of the aircraft.

At the same time, the Rapport III ECM system was installed internally. This involves rewiring the aircraft, and since only a few technicians can work within the confined space of the cockpit and nose section at any one time, the work is slow. Each aircraft spends about six months at the factory, and the modified Falcons are delivered back to the user at a rate of around one a month. At this build standard they are known as Block 10 aircraft. The same factory continues with new production work, Belgian aircraft from the 54th onwards being built to the revised standard.

Deliveries of F-16 aircraft to the Kongelige Danske Flyvevåbnet (Royal Danish Air Force) started on January 28, 1980. The current order is for 46 single-seat F-16A fighters plus 12 two-seat F-16B trainers, and the first squadrons to convert were Esk 727 and 730 at Skrystrup. The former unit was declared

**Left: Belgian Fighting Falcon prepares for an operational task not foreseen in the original US Light Fighter specification – target towing!**

**Below: From 1988 onwards, these Belgian Air Force F-16s will be joined by a follow-on batch of 44 aircraft destined to replace the present Mirage 5 fleet. Despite an attractive offset package devised by Dassault, the FAéB ordered the GD aircraft.**

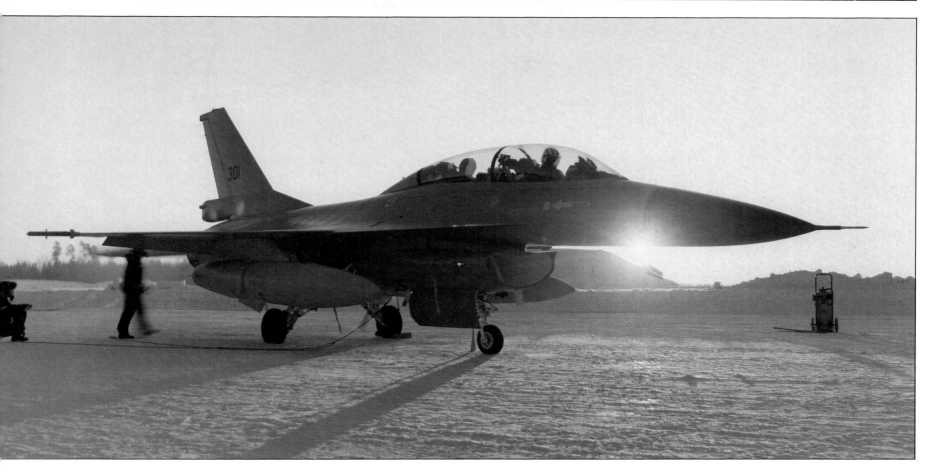

**Above: Norwegian airfields are snow-covered for much of the year, a factor which caused the RNoAF to request braking parachutes in its F-16s.**

operational to NATO on August 26, 1981. Four Danish instructors were trained at Hill AFB, and were assigned to Esk 727 to begin the task of training further instructors.

The next stage of the operation involved the conversion of the most experienced pilots of Esk 727 to the Fighting Falcon. Both squadrons had formerly flown F-100 Super Sabres, and the transition involved the units being split into sub-units designated by the suffixes -100 and -16. While the -100 unit maintained Danish AF combat strength using the F-100, -16 tackled the task of conversion to the GD fighter. As the Fighting Falcon units approached full strength, the Super Sabres were withdrawn from service late in 1982.

Denmark plans to withdraw the Lockheed F-104G Starfighter from operational service in 1984. Esk 723 – one of the two squadrons which currently flies the type – will probably convert to the F-16.

The 1975 agreement between the United States and the four European F-16 operators covered work on 998 aircraft – 348 for the European air arms and 650 for the USAF. This workload is tailing off, but the US has offered further work in return for F-16 follow-on orders being placed in 1983. Denmark looks likely to follow the Belgian lead in placing a follow-on order, but nothing had been announced by mid-1983.

Rather than operate 'twinned' squadrons, the Koninklijke Luchtmacht (Royal Netherlands Air Force) opted to shut down each of the units converting to the Fighting Falcon for the year or so that the transition required. The first F-16 was accepted on June 6, 1979, an operational conversion unit having been set up at Leeuwarden, home base of 322 Sqn, the first to convert from the F-104G. The first instructors were trained at Hill AFB in

the USA. Local pilot and crew training started at Leeuwarden in October 1979, and the first newly-converted pilot joined 322 Sqn in December of the same year.

322 Sqn completed conversion by the end of April 1981. 323 Sqn (also based at Leeuwarden) was the next to be stood down to begin conversion to the Fighting Falcon. A second OCU was set up at Volkel, home base of 306, 311 and 312 Sqns to tackle the conversion of these units, a task which started in 1982.

**Fighting Falcon in the KLu**

Like all European F-16 operators, the KLu plans to use the Fighting Falcon primarily in the close support role. In addition to carrying out air-to-ground attacks, Dutch F-16s will also be used as air-superiority fighters both in the battle area and in the air-defence region allocated to the KLu by NATO.

The last squadron to convert, Nr 306, formerly flew the RF-104G reconnais-

sance aircraft. When re-equipped with Fighting Falcon, it will continue to specialise in reconnaissance, carrying the Oldelft Orpheus recce pod. This role requires only minor adaption of the F-16. Originally deployed on the Starfighter, the Orpheus pod carries five cameras and an infra-red line scanner.

In March 1980 the Netherlands announced plans to increase its F-16 fleet from 102 aircraft (80 F-16A and 22 F-16B) to 213, but the only follow-on announced by the summer of 1983 was for 22 aircraft intended to act as attrition replacements.

Delivery of 60 F-16A and 12 F-16B aircraft to the Kongelige Norske Luftforsvaret (Royal Norwegian Air Force) started on January 25, 1980, and four squadrons will operate the type by 1984. Like its NATO partners, the RNoAF sent an initial batch of personnel to Hill AFB for training. On their return to Norway, these instructors were as-

signed to Skv 332, Norway's first Fighting Falcon unit, for conversion training. By the autumn of 1981, Skv 332 was fully equipped with F-16s and Skv 331 – the first operational unit – had already received many of its aircraft.

Skv 331 and 332 are based at Bodo, and formerly flew F-104G Starfighters. They were followed through the conversion process by Skv 338 from Norland (a former F-5 unit) and Skv 334 from Bodo (formerly an anti-shipping unit whose CF-104D/G fighters were armed with Bullpup missiles). For attacks against surface vessels, RNoAF F-16s will be equipped with the indigenously developed Penguin Mk 3 missile.

Norway's small F-16 force was intended to fulfil a national requirement for a weapon system capable of area defence and anti-invasion strikes, but the numbers ordered were not sufficient to protect all airfields. Funding was allocated under the 1983 defence

**Right: The immaculate condition of this Danish Air Force F-16A, its hangar, mobile tool kit and work platforms would satisfy the most fastidious inspecting officer.**

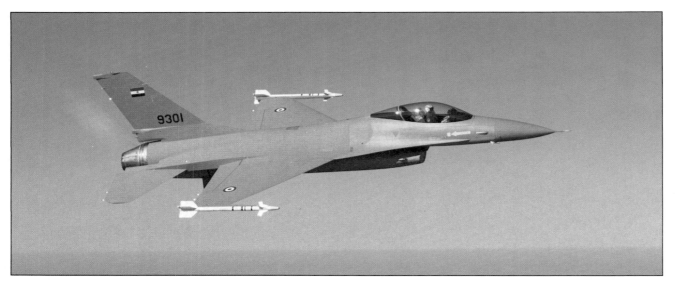

Twartha near Baghdad. Due to become operational in the late summer or early autumn of 1981, this facility was seen as a threat to Israeli security. According to Israeli intelligence, if allowed to 'go critical', the 70MW Osirak reactor would have turned out sufficient plutonium to allow Iraq to construct up to five 20kT nuclear weapons by the mid-1980s.

Timing of the raid was critical. The longer it was delayed, the more complete Osirak would be at the moment of its destruction, and thus the greater the losses in equipment suffered by Iraq. At the same time, it was essential that the raid be conducted before the reactor began operating, lest its destruction released a cloud of intensely radioactive material into the atmosphere.

Selection of the F-16 for the Osirak mission resulted from several factors, including the type's long range, the ground-mapping modes available on the APG-66 radar, and the accuracy of the navigation and attack systems. Eight aircraft formed the strike component of the mission, while six F-15 Eagles flew top cover in order to protect the Fighting Falcons using the longer-range APG-63 radar and AIM-7 Sparrow missiles.

Exact details of the raid have never been published: Israeli accounts contain minimal information, often verging on hagiography rather than combat reporting. The eight aircraft, plus their escort of six F-15s, probably took off from Etzion air base, near Eilat in southern Israel. External tanks were carried and the formation may have begun by topping up from tanker aircraft.

First leg of the flight probably took the formation across southern Jordan and then into Saudi Arabian airspace.

budget for low-level air defence missiles, but this might be used to purchase more F-16s.

## Non-NATO customers

Given the capability of the F-16, further orders for the aircraft were inevitable. On May 7, 1975, both YF-16s were flown to Cecil Field, Jacksonville, Florida to carry out flight demonstrations for the Shah of Iran and King Hussein of Jordan. The programme watched by the monarchs included a mock dogfight between the GD aircraft and an F-4 Phantom.

Iran became the first third-party nation to adopt the F-16. A letter of intent signed by the Imperial Iranian Government on October 27, 1976, covered the procurement of 160 aircraft, and a follow-on buy of a further 140 was also discussed.

Following the Iranian revolution early in 1979, the new Iranian Government cancelled all the massive arms contracts signed by the former Shah, including the F-16 deal. Work on these aircraft had already started, but only minor components had been built. Discussing the cancellation with the author at the time of the announcement, a GD spokesman pointed out that hardware already built could be switched to other customers, and that the likely beneficiary was Israel.

In terms of cost, the loss of the Iranian order had a more marked effect. The likely cost increase for the USAF was estimated at $175,000 per aircraft, while the price rise of European-built examples was predicted to be $129,000 or more per aircraft.

Israel was virtually a captive market for the F-16. After the 1967 arms embargo on the Mirage 5 fleet, Israel was unlikely to place a major order for warplanes with France, and given the importance of the Arab world as a market, it is unlikely that Dassault-Breguet would want the undesirable publicity of another Israeli aircraft deal.

Price information was originally sought on a package of 250 aircraft, and the Tsvah Haganah le Israel – Heyl ha'Avir (Israel Defence Force – Air Force) was reported to have a long-term requirement for a further 150 to 200 examples. In August 1978 Israel announced plans to procure 75 aircraft under a contract valued at around $1·2 billion. This purchase was split between 67 F-16As and eight F-16Bs, and was expected to lead in the longer term to a total purchase of 225 aircraft by the end of the 1980s.

A total of 17 modifications to the Fighting Falcon were requested by the IDFAF: Israeli aircraft would carry weapons not used by other F-16 operators, while IDFAF training and mission-management techniques differed from USAF/NATO practice. Hardware and software had to be modified to meet these specific national requirements.

Deliveries to Israel started on July 2, 1980, at a rate of four per month under a schedule which should have seen the last handed over in November 1981. Flown by US personnel drawn from the 16th Tactical Training Squadron, the first four made the journey from Florida to Israel in 11 hours. An excellent demonstration of the type's long range, this delivery sortie required the use of full external tanks and three in-flight refuellings.

The near-paranoid Israeli rules concerning military security prevent individual IDFAF squadrons or pilots being identified. The identity of the squadron chosen to operate the first Fighting Falcons has never been released officially, but it is known to have a history of pioneering new types. The first Israeli squadron to fly jets, the unit in question equipped with Gloster Meteor F.8 fighters in August 1953, and in 1956 it was the first to receive the Mirage III.

### The Osirak raid

Less than 14 months after entering IDFAF service, the Fighting Falcon went to war. On June 7, 1981, eight were used in a precision air strike against the Osirak nuclear reactor being built at

**Right: As US/Israeli relations grew more strained following the Osirak raid and 1982 invasion of Lebanon, the supply of further F-16s to the IDFAF was repeatedly embargoed.**

Reports published shortly after the raid suggested that during this phase of the mission the Israeli aircrew deliberately set their radios on frequencies normally used by the Jordanian Air Force. Speaking in Arabic and using Jordanian calls signs, they pretended to be Jordanian crews on a training mission.

One report claims that the formation was detected by Saudi radars, but that the aircrew were able to allay suspicions. Probably flying at low level to minimize the risk of interception, the raiders were able to cross the desolate northern part of the country, then turn north into Iraq.

On crossing the Iraqi border, the attackers were fired on by anti-aircraft units, but no hits were scored. Time over the target was 0630, the combination of the early hour and the fact that the day was Sunday being thought to minimize the chance of French technicians being on duty.

### Complete surprise

Tactical surprise was complete, the raiders approaching from the west and reporting some anti-aircraft fire, but no interceptors or SAM launches. The Fighting Falcons attacked in two waves, each consisting of two pairs of aircraft. Prime target was the 105ft (32m) diameter concrete cupola covering the reactor. Individual bomb runs took less than two minutes, the first wave scoring at least two hits with 2,000lb (907kg) Mk 84 bombs.

Early reports suggested that 'smart' bombs were used – perhaps Texas Instruments Paveway LGBs guided by Pave Spike designator pod – but Israeli spokesmen claimed that 'iron' bombs were used in conjunction with what IDFAF commander General David Ivri described as 'a new technique ... based on the excellence of our pilots'.

The reactor was badly damaged, the protective dome collapsing and burying the complex in rubble, while laboratories and other facilities were also damaged and one French technician was killed. The second wave is reported not to have bombed. The attackers were not engaged during the return flight, which took them westwards, back across Jordan and into Israeli airspace. The Reagan administration told Congress that the raid may have been a 'substantial violation' of US/Israeli mutual defense agreements, and placed a temporary embargo on F-16 deliveries to the IDFAF.

Delivery of further F-16s was temporarily embargoed once again on July 17, 1981, following a week-long series of attacks on Palestinian bases in the Lebanon. At this point 53 aircraft had been delivered, and ten more were due to begin their flight to Israel that day. Delivery of all 75 aircraft to Israel was eventually completed by the end of 1981. In May 1982 the US Congress was told that the Reagan Administration intended to supply a further 75 F-16s to the IDFAF, with deliveries starting in 1985.

The spring and summer of 1982 saw IDFAF Fighting Falcons in action once again. In the course of air combat over the Bekaa valley in Lebanon the Israeli Air Force claimed the destruction of 92 Syrian fighters, more than half of which were MiG-23 Floggers. In this air-to-air fighting the F-16 emerged as the top-scoring 'MiG-killer', downing 44 Syrian warplanes, while the F-15 accounted for a further 40. Most of the kills were

scored using the AIM-9L 'all-aspect' version of Sidewinder.

Aircraft most commonly met in combat by the Israeli pilots were the MiG-21, MiG-23 and Su-22. Syrian tactics were poor, according to the Israeli pilots, with little evidence of careful pre-flight planning. There was no shortage of bravery, however – wave upon wave of Syrian aircraft rushed into combat despite their heavy losses.

In an interview with the magazine *Flight International*, an unidentified senior Israeli officer ascribed the Syrian loss rate to a combination of shortcomings in the command structure and in the individual aircrew. "In the 1973 war the Syrian pilots fought aggressively, this time it was different ... they could have flown the best fighter in the world, but if they flew the way they were flying, we would have shot them down. It wasn't the equipment at fault, but their tactics ... They fired missiles, they fought, but in a peculiar way ... in our opinion, they acted without tactical sense." One immediate result of this Israeli success was yet another temporary embargo on Fighting Falcon deliveries, with President Reagan banning the supply of the follow-on batch of aircraft. This was duly lifted in May 1983.

On June 25, 1980, Egypt signed a letter of agreement covering the supply of 40 F-16s. The deal was worth more than $960 million and included the 40 aircraft, ten spare F100 engines, and ordnance including 600 Maverick rounds, 500lb (227kg) and 1,000lb (454kg) bombs and 20mm cannon ammunition. Also included were a simulator plus other support equipment and manuals.

Egypt originally wanted the F-15, and despite having the F-16 on order still wanted the Eagle, presumably as part of a 'Hi-Lo' mix. By 1980 it was obvious that the McDonnell Douglas warplane was too expensive for Egypt's limited budget and the likely level of US military credit available, so this plan was abandoned, at least for the time being.

### Diversions to Egypt

Growing unserviceability of Soviet-supplied warplanes made early delivery of the Fighting Falcon essential, and in order to meet Egyptian requests that deliveries be speeded up 30 examples were diverted from the USAF. Between December 1981 and May 1983 monthly deliveries to the USAF were cut from 15 aircraft to around 13. The remaining ten EAF F-16s were built from scratch as export aircraft.

Aircraft for the Egyptian Air Force started down the production line in 1981, and all 40 were due to be delivered by early 1984. Egyptian aircraft are F-16A & B standard and not equipped with the MSIP avionics or provision

for AMRAAM missiles. The EAF would like to have the Hughes missile, but any agreement covering its supply would have to form part of a future and separate agreement.

The current mixture of US, French, Soviet and Chinese equipment deployed by Egypt clearly places great strain on that nation's IFF systems. All EAF fighters, including the F-16 and Soviet types, are equipped with IFF units developed and supplied by Teledyne.

Egypt has a total requirement for 120 F-16s to replace part of the aging fleet of Soviet-supplied MiGs and Sukhois. Given the high cost of Western defence equipment compared to Soviet products, the EAF will be unable to replace Fishbeds and Fitters on a one-for-one basis, so the nominal size of the service will decline during the 1980s.

Being short of modern aircraft, Egypt uses the Fighting Falcon for both air defence and ground attack. The Egyptian Air Force sees an eventual need for up to 150 examples, and has already requested a second batch of 40. Even before the first examples of the F-16 were operational in Egypt, the US Defense Department was planning to allow Egypt to place a follow-on order. As part of a $1,300 million package of military sales credits for Egypt requested from Congress in 1982, the Pentagon wanted to supply a further 40

aircraft, with deliveries beginning in 1985. An agreement covering the supply of these follow-on aircraft was signed in May 1982. The 40 aircraft in this second batch will be delivered between late 1985 and the autumn of 1987.

Having built up experience in the construction of modern aircraft by assembling Alpha Jets for the Egyptian Air Force, Egyptian industry is keen to co-produce more advanced types. Both the F-16/79 and the F-20 have been proposed as possible successors, but the problem of funding such a programme seems immense: a price tag of $2,000 million has been estimated.

### F-16s for Korea

President Carter's idealistic plan, announced in 1977, to withdraw 39,000 US troops from South Korea was soon to be suspended as the 1970s drew to a close, but triggered off that nation's equipment upgrading plans. A requirement for 100 new fighters was identified, and US approval for the purchase of 72 aircraft was requested in 1979.

**Below: Painted with temporary US markings and loaded with external tanks, a Fighting Falcon begins the long trip which will end some 11 hours later in delivery to the Israeli Defence Force – Air Force.**

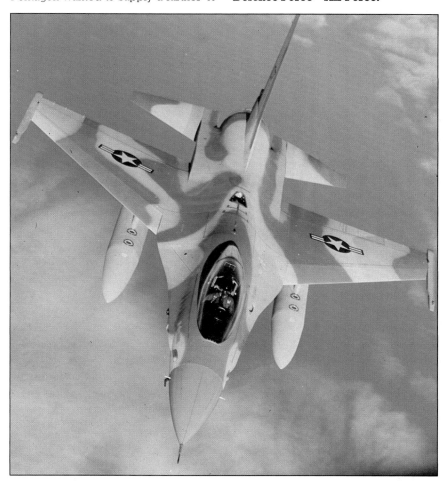

**Right: Israeli Fighting Falcon in its delivery paint scheme. Squadron insignia added to the aircraft since then are deleted from all official photographs.**

The first USAF F-16s to be deployed to South Korea arrived in August 1981, but the South Korean government signed a letter of offer for 36 aircraft of its own at the end of that year. Worth $930 million, the deal covered 30 single-seat and six two-seat aircraft, with deliveries beginning in February 1986 at a rate of one per month. It also covered spares, training and technical assistance.

The supply of advanced warplanes to Pakistan was clearly a politically sensitive issue, plans to supply the Vought A-7 Corsair II having been abandoned in the mid-1970s when Pakistan insisted on proceeding with plans to purchase a nuclear fuel re-processing plant from France – a possible key step along the route to developing indigenous nuclear weapons. Following the Soviet intervention in Afghanistan, however, the US State Department sanctioned the supply of 40 F-16s, Pakistan becoming the ninth nation to adopt the type when contracts were signed in December 1981.

Pakistan is to get 40 aircraft, the first six of which were delivered at the end of 1982, while the remainder are covered by a separate contract. The Fighting Falcon will probably replace part of the current fleet of Shenyang F-6 Farmers (Chinese-built MiG-19s).

Next customer for the Fighting Falcon was the Fuerzas Aéreas Venezolanas (Venezuelan Air Forces), which needed to replace the elderly Mirage IIIE fighters operated by Esc 34 at Palo Negro. Venezuela's proposed order for 16 single-seat and eight two-seat aircraft was sent to the US Congress for formal approval at the end of 1981, and the contract was signed in May 1982. Deliveries are due to begin in the autumn of 1983, with six aircraft being delivered in that year and six in 1984. The remaining 24 should be delivered in 1985.

## Other evaluations

To date, the Fighting Falcon has attracted no other export orders, but this has not been due to any lack of marketing effort. The aircraft was a candidate in several fighter evaluations of the late 1970s and early 1980s, and is under consideration by several nations. For convenience, these current evaluations and 'also-rans' are listed below by country and in alphabetical order.

Australia's requirement for a Mirage IIIO replacement called for the procurement of up to 160 aircraft, and GD attempted to create an attractive package of F-16 work for Australian industry, despite the inexperience of the latter. Final assembly of the aircraft in-country was proposed, although the modest size (75) of the planned order made the economies of such a move questionable. Company estimates suggested that at least 150 aircraft would have to be assembled to justify the initial capital costs.

In both the Canadian and Australian fighter-selection competitions, the F-16 has lost out to the larger, twin-engined McDonnell Douglas F/A-18A Hornet. The reasons cited were generally those of genuine all-weather avionics in the standard aircraft, plus the extra safety of the twin-engine propulsion system. The Australian evaluation did highlight the lower overall programme cost of the GD fighter, although it suggested that the support and attrition costs over the lifetime of the planned fleet might substantially reduce the difference.

A four-man Österreichische Luftstreitkräfte (Austrian Air Force) team evaluated the F-16A in 1980. During one test the aircraft took off just under two minutes after engine start, reaching Mach 2 at 40,000ft (14,000m) within six minutes of brake release. Theoretical winner of this evaluation was the Dassault-Breguet Mirage 50, but plans to place an order have been suspended. Air defence is not highly placed in the Austrian government's list of priorities.

Initial goal of the Canadian Armed Forces was to select its next fighter in December 1977, and to begin deployment of the chosen aircraft in 1980. At least 120 were wanted, with perhaps a further 200 being ordered in the longer term. At the end of a three-year study, Canada finally selected the F/A-18 in April 1980. Factors influencing the choice included the greater safety offered by a twin-engined design, the higher performance of the F/A-18 systems and the avionics growth space.

Greece, which attempts to maintain a close military balance with Turkey, requested data on a possible procurement of 150–200 F-16s. The F-16 was one candidate in the Helliniki Aeroporía (Greek Air Force) search for a new fighter, being evaluated in competition with the F/A-18, F-18L, Mirage 2000 and Tornado. A total of 100 aircraft are needed, with a possible follow-on order for 30 more, but selection of the winner has been long delayed and no decision had been announced by mid-1983. Reports in the local press favoured the F-18L and Tornado, but the US government is thought to favour an F-16 deal, since the last-named aircraft could also be supplied to Turkey, maintaining the local military balance.

## Japan chooses F-15

Japan's defence budget is not over-lavish. When 'shopping' for a new fighter in the late 1970s, the Nihon Koku Jieitai (Japan Air Self-Defense Force) appreciated the need to obtain the most effective force which the limited funding would permit. What was required was not only a new fighter, but also an early-warning and control system.

Japan evaluated the F-14, F-15 and F-16: the last could have allowed a larger fleet, but an order was finally placed for 123 F-15 Eagle fighters to be built under licence by Mitsubishi.

In the autumn of 1982 it seemed the Fuerza Aérea del Peru (Peruvian Air Force) might become the first South American FX customer. Data on price and availability of the F-16/79 were requested, and the FAP was thought likely to acquire 26 examples. After considering a subsequent US offer, Peru opted later the same year to order 24 Mirage 2000 fighters for delivery beginning in late 1984.

During negotiations held in the late 1970s over the future of US bases on Spanish territory, the Spanish government asked for 72 F-16s or aircraft of similar performance to be supplied.

The F-16 was clearly a front runner in the Spanish FACA (Futuro Avion de Combate y Ataque, or future fighter and attack aircraft) competition, being evaluated against the Mirage 2000, F/A-18 and Northrop F-18L. The Ejército del Aire Español (Spanish Air Force) wanted 144 aircraft, but by mid-1981 the maximum number likely to be affordable had fallen to 104. Selection of the F/A-18 was announced in July 1982, but only 82 examples could be afforded. The planned procurement was reviewed in 1983, a limited re-evaluation of the competing types being carried out before a final decision to acquire 72 F/A-18 Hornets was announced.

A Saudi Arabian requirement for 150 lightweight fighters for interception duties was reported in 1977. Despite the subsequent purchase of 60 McDonnell Douglas F-15 Eagles by the Al Quwwat al Jawwiya as Sa'udiya (Royal Saudi Air Force) under the Peace Sun programme, the US government still considers Saudi Arabia a potential customer for FX-class fighters.

With the growing diplomatic ties between the US and China in the 1970s, Taiwan found itself increasingly isolated in diplomatic terms. The Air Force wanted the F-16, but the range of the GD aircraft would have given the Fighting Falcon a significant strike capability against the Chinese mainland. Supply of the F-16, F-16/79 or Northrop F-20 was vetoed by the US government – largely as a result of political pressure from the People's Republic of China – so Chung-kuo Kung Chuan (Chinese Nationalist Air Force) re-equipment plans are now based on the F-5E Tiger.

During the late 1970s and early 1980s, a number of ambitious plans were conceived by the Turkish government in its attempts to set up a viable national aerospace industry. A requirement for 150 to 200 F-16s was discussed with the US, but serious study of this was hampered by the arms embargo enforced by the US following the invasion of Cyprus in 1974, and by Turkey's acute shortage of funds for new equipment. The equipment finally adopted by the Türk Hava Kuvvetleri (Turkish Air Force) is likely to be supplied as US military aid, and will probably be influenced by the final choice of fighter made by Greece. The US Government will almost certainly ensure that a military balance in terms of quality and quantity of equipment is maintained between these rival air arms.

**Right: The black radome on this Royal Netherlands Air Force F-16A of 308 Sqn identifies the aircraft as an early production example. Under the Pacer Loft programme these are being updated to Block 15 standard.**

**Right: F-16A of the 35th TFS, 8th TFW – the 'Wolf Pack' – from Kunsan Air Base, South Korea. Note the wolf's head insignia, which appears on both sides of the fuselage.**

**Right: Royal Norwegian Air Force F-16s are finished in an overall grey paint scheme, and carry the fuselage national markings below the aft section of the canopy.**

**Right and below: The emblem on the intake of this USAF Fighting Falcon identifies it as an aircraft of the 4th Tactical Fighter Squadron, 388th TFW, based at Hill AFB, Utah.**

# Performance and Handling

**Ready for takeoff on an air-combat mission with no external tanks, Fighting Falcon tips the scales at around half the weight of an F-4 or F-15 tasked with a similar mission. Even by the standards of classic lightweight designs such as the MiG-21 Fishbed and Dassault-Breguet Mirage III, the F-16 is still a light fighter, weighing about one third more than the Soviet fighter and twelve per cent more than the Dassault delta. The GD aircraft matches its light weight with combat performance which the Mirage or MiG pilot can only dream about and a weapon delivery accuracy better than that of the F-111.**

A lightly loaded F-16 with full internal fuel has a thrust-to-weight ratio of just over 1:1 in full afterburner. Working with the lightweight YF-16 prototypes, GD test pilots carried out pre-takeoff engine and system checks at 80 per cent power. Application of full afterburning power would have caused the wheels to slide.

Fighting Falcon begins its take-off roll with the wing leading and trailing-edge flaps positioned 2deg up and 20deg down respectively. After brake release, the aircraft quickly picks up speed. Rotation is usually at around 125kt, liftoff at around 140kt.

When Robert Ropelewski of *Aviation Week* flew the F-16B for the first time in 1979, GD Chief test pilot Neil Anderson was able to demonstrate the takeoff performance: "Anderson ... rotated the nose upwards, stopping at 60deg pitch as the aircraft began climbing out". Given the 30deg reclining tilt of the Fighting Falcon ejection seat, this climb angle meant that the torsos of the two pilots were literally horizontal. The F-16 can climb vertically, but this would result in the pilot hanging head-down in his seat.

"Acceleration continued, even in that attitude", reported Ropelewski, "the aircraft passing through 170kt about 30 seconds after brake release. A wing-over manoeuvre was used to level the aircraft at around 8,000ft (2,450m) altitude, still within the length of the Carswell (AFB) runway. A USAF Northrop T-38 chase aircraft which had started its takeoff roll on the same runway five seconds after the F-16 was just lifting off the runway below."

When the undercarriage is retracted the leading edge changes to 20deg down, while the gain of the flight-control system is doubled to reach its normal flight value. (The 50 per cent reduction while on the ground was incorporated as a result of the inadvertent first flight of the original YF-16 prototype). Throughout the mission the flight-control system remains at full gain, except when the door which covers the refuelling receptacle is opened. The latter operation reduce the control response in pitch and roll by an amount designed to make the aircraft 'less nervous', during the approach to the tanker, refuelling and subsequent separation.

One of the most novel features of the F-16 cockpit is the sidestick controller used in place of the traditional control column. This is located on the starboard side of the cockpit, and incorporates an adjustable armrest mounted on the cockpit wall. This is essential in high-g flight conditions, and includes an optional wrist rest which may be folded

back against the wall if not required.

The original pattern of sidestick controller did not move, but was force sensitive only. Although effective, this scheme provided no indication to the pilot of when maximum input was being demanded. To avoid sprained wrists in the excitement of high-g manoeuvres, the USAF decided to allow the definitive design of stick a few millimetres of movement to provide the required degree of 'feedback' to the pilot. The rudder pedals have around 0.5in (1cm) of movement.

The flight-control system ensures that the pilot cannot over-stress the airframe. No matter how hard he operates the controls, the angle of attack and load factor are limited, ensuring that he cannot demand more than 25deg angle of attack or 9g load factor.

In practice, the 9g figure is probably close to the limit that the human body can take while performing a useful military mission. In conventional cockpits, pilots often experience tunnel vision – commonly known as grey-out – at levels of around 6 or 7g, but the semi-reclining seat of the F-16 seems to extend this limit by up to 2g. *Aviation Week's* Robert Ropelewski noted no vision problems at manoeuvres of 8g or more, despite having had grey-out at around 7g in other aircraft.

**Above: Even in dry thrust the F-16 is capable of impressive aerobatics. In combat, the added impetus of the afterburner offers the pilot 'brute force' solutions to any desired manoeuvre, while his opponent might have to conserve energy.**

**Right: The superb visibility of the F-16's canopy is illustrated by this view of aircraft from the 8th TFW. If the pilot looked round he would be able to see his own vertical stabilizer.**

The brisk acceleration of the F-16 is a feature which has attracted much comment from pilots. Neil Anderson quotes one of the USAF pilots who tested the YF-16 as saying that flying the F-16 was '... like riding on top of a telegraph pole. Every time you light the afterburner, you are a little nervous that it is going to run out from under you'.

Any feeling that the pilot rides on top of the Fighting Falcon rather than within it is heightened by a bulbous canopy large enough to allow the pilot to look over his shoulder and observe his vertical stabilizer and see whether or not he is leaving a con-trial. Pilots used to the more traditional pattern of low-drag canopy used on such aircraft as the F-4 or A-7 are likely to feel somewhat exposed. At relatively modest bank

6 Vertical roll

5 8g+ high-performance turn

4 Idle power vertical reversal

1 Takeoff loop

3 Low-speed vertical climb

2 Level roll

**Above: Neil Anderson (left), Chief Test Pilot at General Dynamics, played a major role in the F-16 programme. Colleague James McKinney (right) flew the aircraft during the 1979 and 1981 Paris Air Shows.**

**Left: This composite diagram illustrates some of the manoeuvres flown by the F-16 at Farnborough and Paris Air Shows during the late 1970s.**

angles the pilot is able to look vertically downward at the terrain below, while the absence of canopy frames in the forward field of view removes the reference points by which pilots instinctively position the horizon during normal flight. During initial Fighting Falcon sorties, new pilots are recommended to fly by instruments until they become accustomed to the external view.

In high-speed cruise the wing leading and trailing-edge flaps are positioned 2deg above centre. Should the pilot attempt maximum-rate manoeuvres, the leading edge will move to 25deg down and the trailing edge will move to neutral. Vortexes generated by the leading-edge strakes play a significant part in improving the handling of the Fighting Falcon, producing improved

**Above: Visibility from the cockpit of the F-16 is greatly superior to that from the MiG-21bis.**

**Left: F-16B two-seater flies an impressive-looking 9g climbing turn.**

airflow over the wings and vertical tail. Lift, pitch and directional stability are all improved, while buffet intensity is reduced. Hard manoeuvring at high supersonic speeds can result in some buffeting, according to GD, but for most of the performance envelope Fighting Falcon is buffet-free. Transition through the transonic region is smooth, with only a slight buffeting as speed is increased through Mach 0.95.

Full details of the performance of the F-16A and C had not been released by June 1983. Unclassified brochures on the J79-powered version include the manoeuvre-capability charts reproduced here, but the equivalent charts for the F-16 bear no numerical data. During test flights, however, the F-16 has been flown at speeds in excess of Mach 2, and at altitudes greater than 60,000ft (18,300m). Thanks to the massive thrust of the F100, Fighting Falcon can climb at virtually any airspeed.

**Performance of the F-16A compared with that of the MiG-21bis third-generation version of the Fishbed fighter. The diagrams assume a speed of Mach 0.85 at sea level (above) and 20,000ft (6,000m) (right). In all cases turning performance, acceleration and rate of climb are superior to those of the MiG.**

Few fighters will be able to out-turn the Fighting Falcon. Flown in a 325–350kt turn against an F-4, a YF-16 prototype was able to carry out a full 360deg turn by the time the older fighter had managed some 240–250deg. Even at sea level the F-16 is able to out-turn the Mikoyan MiG-21bis. In terms of rate of climb, acceleration and turning performance, Fighting Falcon easily exceeds the performance of the Soviet fighter at altitudes of up to 30,000ft (9,000m). Comparative date for greater altitudes is not available.

According to one unclassified chart (produced by a rival US company) detailing comparative aircraft performance, maximum instantaneous turn rate of Fighting Falcon is just over 20deg/sec – virtually the same as that of the F-14 Tomcat and F-20 Tigershark. This figure is marginally bettered only by the Mirage 2000 and F/A-18 Hornet, and is a 50 per cent improvement over that associated with older types such as the Mirage III, F-4 Phantom and F-5E.

According to the RNethAF, the F-16 is "unbeatable" in simulated air combat. By early 1981 the aircraft had been flown against USAFE F-15 Eagles from Bitburg and Soesterberg in West Germany, and against RNethAF Mirage 5B fighters. The radar gave the service a level of look-down performance totally lacking in earlier types such as the F-104G.

Fighting Falcon is also an effective strike aircraft. Even at high speed and low altitude, air turbulence does create significant aircraft instability. Ropelewski has reported flying at 600kts at 100ft (30m) altitude with impressive results. "The aircraft was flyable hands-off, with no indication of gust upsets or even the slightest vertical or lateral accelerations."

During bombing practice, F-16 crews have displayed accuracies well above those obtained with earlier tactical fighters. According to the USAF, 2,000lb (907kg) iron bombs can be dropped within 30ft (9m) of a target, compared

**Above: Precise performance details of the F-16A are classified, but this chart shows the F-16/79's instantaneous manoeuvre capability.**

**Above: Sustained manoeuvre capability of the F-16/79 is lower than the instantaneous capability, but the ability to sustain 7g is available in the most likely combat conditions.**

**Right: Con-trails forming from the strakes of this F-16 trace the path of the vortexes passing over the wing. These streams of energized air greatly enhance flying qualities.**

**Above: Despite its relatively large wing area, the Fighting Falcon offers pilots a smooth ride at low altitudes and high air speeds, essential qualities for the strike role.**

with the 150ft (45m) typical using the F-4. The best crews of the Korean-based 8th TFW were scoring CEPs (circular error probable) of 9ft (2.74m) during 10deg diving attacks, while the average figure for the unit was 35ft (11m). Given this sort of accuracy, some pilots argue, there is no need to carry guided missiles or 'smart' bombs unless small hard targets such as bridges are to be attacked.

In substituting the GE J79 turbojet in place of the F100 to create the F-16/79 FX export fighter, GD has paid some performance penalty. Two years after his F-16B sortie, Ropelewski was able to fly the F-16/79 and noted a lower takeoff performance. "Acceleration is slower than with the F100 engine and the initial climb attitude is less impressive – in the neighbourhood of 30deg pitch compared with around 60deg for the standard aircraft – in a typical air-to-air configuration."

As the undercarriage is lowered prior to landing, the wing leading and trailing-edge flaps return to the 15 & 20deg down high-lift configuration used for the initial climb, while control sensitivity is reduced by 50 per cent to eliminate any possibility of over-correction.

Typical approach speed is around 125kt, with the aircraft touching down at or just below 120kt. After landing the nose is held up at an angle of 13deg to obtain aerodynamic braking, the nosewheel not being lowered until speed has dropped to around 100kt. Typical landing runs at an aircraft weight of

**Right: In seeking a replacement for the ageing Northrop T-38 Talon, the USAF's Thunderbirds display team finally adopted the Fighting Falcon. It was first used during the 1983 season.**

20,000lb (9,000kg) are around 3,000ft (900m) on dry asphalt or concrete.

The problem of dead-stick landing is of concern to the pilot of any 'hot' single-engined aircraft. The earlier F-104G Starfighter had been particularly unforgiving in this respect, since the wing flaps were blown with engine air to improve lift. To make sure that the Fighting Falcon driver would have confidence in his aircraft should the engine fail, a series of dead-stick landing trials were carried out using the YF-16 prototypes. Initial tests showed that the aircraft could glide at around 150kt with undercarriage and flaps down, but a figure of 170kt was later chosen.

**Below: Without its electronic fly-by-wire system the F-16 would not be controllable.**

# Experimental Variants

**Like most successful designs, the F-16 has the potential for development into more advanced versions. Few aircraft can have been subjected to quite so many re-engining and rebuild programmes at such an early stage of their career: within ten years of the first flight by a prototype experimental versions have included an aircraft able to taxi on rain-drenched soil, experimental delta-winged variants, CCV configurations pioneering new ways to fly, forward-swept wings and even a proposed vectored-thrust STOVL model. One thing is certain – the story is unlikely to stop with the aircraft described here.**

Fighting Falcon has been used as a testbed for several experimental programmes. In some cases the aircraft was simply a convenient guinea-pig, but other projects involved drastic rebuilds and could lead to more advanced future versions of the F-16.

One of the YF-16 prototypes was used in 1982 to test a novel method of operating high-performance aircraft from damaged airfields. The USAF asked Vehicle System Development Corporation of California to devise a method of allowing jet fighters to be taxied over rough or soft ground. This would allow

**Below: Fighting Falcon of the future? Equipped with intake-mounted canards and a MiG-21 style dorsal spine, the ATFI/F-16 is engaged in research which could lead to entirely new types of combat manoeuvre.**

aircraft trapped in hardened shelters at bases attacked by anti-airfield weapons such as JP233 to be taken from their shelters and taxied to a takeoff site without using the damaged or mined taxiways.

### Wrap-around tracks
The solution devised was to fit wrap-around tracks to the nose and main wheels. These effectively widened and lengthened the 'footprint' of each wheel, reducing ground pressure and, consequently, the chance of the aircraft bogging down in soft terrain. Normal ground pressure of an F-16 is around 275lb/sq in (19kg/sq cm), but the use of the FloTrak wrap-arounds reduces this to just under 80lb/sq in (5·5kg/sq cm). During trials held at Wright-Patterson AFB, Ohio, a YF-16 fitted with FloTraks was able to taxi over rough ground at

speeds of up to 35kt, and was towed across rain-soaked soft ground. At one point during the latter test the wheels of the towing tractor began to sink into the waterlogged soil, but the YF-16 was still free to move.

One of the YF-16 prototypes was rebuilt in the mid-1970s as part of the USAF Flight Dynamics Laboratory Control-Configured Vehicle (CCV) programme. Canard surfaces were added beneath the air intake, one on each side of the nose wheel, the fuel system was modified to allow greater control over the position of the aircraft centre of gravity, and the flight-control system was modified to allow the aircraft to be manoeuvred in ways not possible with conventional controls.

In a normal aircraft, movements in one plane are often related to movements in another. For example, in order

**Above: The FloTrak wrap-around may look clumsy if not downright agricultural, but trials have shown that with its aid an F-16 could be towed across waterlogged ground, or taxied over a rough field.**

to turn, a conventional aircraft must bank. On the YF-16/CCV, movements are fully independent or 'decoupled'. The aircraft can rise or fall using direct lift, move laterally by direct side force, or yaw, pitch or roll independently of direction of flight.

GD test pilot David J. Thigpen flew the modified aircraft in its new configuration for the first time on March 16, 1976, starting what was scheduled to be a programme of 85 flights. While coming in to land at the end of the 29th CCV test mission on June 24, 1976, the aircraft suffered a loss of engine power while still some half a mile from touch-down. Thigpen brought the aircraft down in a rough landing, but the under-carriage collapsed under the strain. Subsequent repairs took more than six months, flights resuming in the spring of 1977.

The flight-test programme was com-pleted by the end of July of that year. After 125 hours of experimental flying (87 flights), the YF-16/CCV proved that the new degrees of freedom such as fuselage pointing measurably improved mission effectiveness, and that future aircraft incorporating CCV technology could be designed to be smaller, light-er, less expensive and more manoeuvr-able than conventional types.

### The AFTI/F-16

Advances in electronic technology re-sulting from digital systems and large-scale integrated circuits suggest that future fighters will be able to incorpor-ate new types of flight-control and nav/attack systems. To evaluate these, the USAF has devised the Advanced Fight-er Technology Integration (AFTI) pro-gramme. This uses a heavily modified F-16 as a testbed, GD having been awarded a contract on December 26, 1978, to rebuild one of the full-scale development F-16s. The aircraft was handed over to the company in March 1980.

The AFTI/F-16 is immediately recog-nizable by the presence of intake-mounted canard surfaces and a dorsal spine similar to that fitted to third-generation MiG-21s. The latter modi-fication provides the internal volume needed to house flight-test equipment. The AFTI/F-16 has a triplex digital flight-control system which will give the pilot CCV-type freedom of manoeuvre. All movements are fully decoupled.

First flight of the modified aircraft was delayed by software problems, but finally took place at Fort Worth on July 10, 1982. The first three test flights were carried out at Fort Worth by GD pilots, and the aircraft was then flown to Ed-wards AFB, California, to begin a two-year programme of 275 test flights.

The first year of flying explored the unorthodox flight modes such as fusel-age pointing and direct-force trans-lation. Early sorties checked aircraft behaviour over a large portion of the performance envelope, before work began on proving the digital flight con-trol system and the new degrees of freedom which it permits.

Pilots will explore the effects of adding decoupled degrees of freedom to normal flight, determining how the

new freedom of manoeuvre can best be used, and how unconventional motions and attitudes affect the pilot. If some manoeuvres cause vertigo or nausea in pilots, they will be of little use in combat, so this type of man-machine interaction must be explored. The USAF anticipates that trials will confirm that normal coupled flight modes are best for most of a sortie, handling the major changes to the flight path. Decoupled modes will probably be reserved for 'fine-trimming' aircraft position in simu-lated combat.

At the end of this phase, the aircraft will be returned to Fort Worth for furth-er updating, so that integrated flight and fire-control tests can begin. This will involve the installation of the Automatic Manoeuvring Attack System (AMAS), whose main components are a Westing-house sensor pod containing a FLIR

sensor and laser rangefinder, a helmet-mounted sight, digital fire-control com-puter, radar altimeter and a Standard Avionics-Integrated Fuzing (SAIF) unit.

The sensor pod will be mounted in the port wing root, and will share the digital programmable signal processor of the APG-66 radar. In operational use, the pod may be slaved to the radar, helmet sight, or inertial navigation system so that targets detected by the latter can be tracked by passive infra-red means. This will reduce the amount of time during which the aircraft must transmit. The pod may also be used to acquire targets independently. Data from the FLIR will be passed in turn to the integrated flight/fire-control system, which will generate the commands needed to steer the aircraft automati-cally towards the target.

The two years of test flying will be

**Above: Seen from this angle the F-16/XL bears a distinct resemblance to Fort Worth's biggest delta – the Convair B-58 Hustler. Note how the stores are mounted close to the underside of the wing.**

intensive, making use of flight-test facili-ties originally devised for the Space Shuttle programme. These will allow data from the aircraft to be processed in real time, so that the results of a sortie will be available before the aircraft has landed. Testing is due to culminate in a tactical evaluation during a Red Flag exercise at Nellis AFB, Nevada.

In 1980, news of a new and drastically modified F-16 variant was leaked to the US technical press. Designated SCAMP (Supersonic Cruise and Manoeuvring Prototype), this was based on studies carried out by GD between 1976 and

**Below: First F-16 to explore the strange world of decoupled flight movements was the YF-16/CCV. A series of 87 flights by the rebuilt prototype the mid-1970s paved the way for the more recent AFTI/F-16.**

## New ways to fly

**To fly upward, a conventional aircraft would have to raise its nose through the angle of attack shown between the arrows. The AFTI/F-16 simply rises in 'vertical translation'.**

**Lateral translation is similar to vertical translation: the aircraft can move sideways without yawing the nose through the angle shown.**

**Using direct lift the aircraft can climb or descend while maintaining an unchanging angle of attack – a useful method of trimming the flight path during weapon delivery.**

**Direct sideforce turns do not involve rolling the aircraft – the pilot may turn his mount in one plane only, as if taxying on the ground.**

**When carrying out air-to-air gun attacks, an AFTI/F-16 is able to raise or lower its nose without affecting the flight path. This is termed pitch-axis pointing.**

**Like pitch-axis pointing, yaw-axis pointing allows the nose to be moved without changing the direction of flight.**

1980, and featured a 'cranked' delta wing, a configuration proposed to the USAF by GD in February 1980. Although the programme was at this stage a private venture by the manufacturer, the USAF did provide support, and the third and sixth full-scale development F-16s were returned to GD in the summer of 1981 for conversion to the new configuration.

Given the large production base of the F-16, GD designers tried to capitalize on existing components and experience in order to reduce the potential cost of the new variant. Wings and horizontal tail account for about 11 per cent of the total cost of the F-16, and these are the main all-new components in what was now designated the F-16XL. Although the rebuild did involve a modest fuselage stretch, the new designation did not, as some humorists suggested, stand for 'Xtra Length'!

Despite the significant external differences between the F-16A and the F-16XL, the airframe of the latter has more than 70 per cent commonality with the standard fighter. If a production version were to be ordered by the USAF, this would probably have MSIP-standard avionics, including the modified radar and LANTIRN.

### F-16XL flight tests

First flight of the F-16XL took place at Fort Worth on July 15, 1982. This first sortie was all-subsonic, the aircraft reaching a top speed of Mach 0·9, a height of 30,000ft (9,000m), a maximum load factor of 3g and 20deg of angle of attack. At takeoff the angle of attack was 8deg, rising to 10deg at landing. Both values are well below those associated with traditional delta designs. Test pilot Jim McKinney reported that handling was 'very different' from that of the basic F-16, offering a 'solid ride'.

Following a small number of flights, the aircraft was transferred to Edwards AFB to begin a joint USAF/GD trials programme. Due to run for 240 flights over a period of nine months, this exercise involved both prototypes – the single-seat F100-powered version and the later GE F110-powered two-seater. Tests assessed the 'ride' which the aircraft offers at low level, and the use of high-speed tactics for defense penetration without the use of afterburner.

The second F-16XL is a two-seat rebuild of a full-scale development F-16A which was damaged in a landing accident. Ground proof-load tests of this aircraft suggested that the aft wing spar would fail at around 85 per cent of the planned limit, so the centre 22in (56cm) section of aluminium spar was replaced by a steel component.

First flight of the second F-16XL took place on October 29, 1982, again from Fort Worth. This aircraft, powered by the GE F110 turbofan, reached Mach 1.4 on its first sortie, with test pilot Alex Wolf in the front cockpit and Jim McKinney in the rear.

During the first 53 hours of F-16XL flight tests a total of seven GD and USAF pilots flew the aircraft. Highlights of this first period of testing included speeds approaching Mach 2·0 and altitudes of up to 50,000ft (15,240m). The aircraft refuelled from a KC-135 tanker, reached a speed of Mach 1·2 while carrying 12 Mk 82 bombs, and ripple-released the same ordnance load during dropping tests. After a brief grounding while further vibration trials were carried out and a braking parachute was installed, the aircraft began a series of stability and control tests, including an exploration of high angles of attack.

An evaluation of the two cranked-wing F-16XL prototypes by the USAF began in the summer of 1982. The FY 1983 budget included \$21 million to cover the cost of the two F-16XL prototypes, as well as \$57 million for the rebuilding of an F-15 Eagle fighter to the proposed F-15E strike configuration.

At one time the existence of the F-16 seemed to threaten USAF plans to develop a heavy strike fighter based on the F-15. The GAO asked the service in the summer of 1981 to justify its announced need for dedicated strike versions of the McDonnell-Douglas fighter and the F-16. Throughout the tests, the USAF was careful to avoid suggestions that the aircraft were in competitive evaluation, but the US Congress will not allow the USAF to buy both types.

One exotic F-16 variant which never left the Fort Worth drawing boards was the SFW/F-16 developed for the Defense Advanced Research Projects Agency (DARPA) forward-swept wing programme. Forward-swept wings offer good low-speed handling characteristics and low drag, but are very difficult to manufacture using conventional technology. The use of advanced composite materials allows the wing to be made strong enough to prevent the unwanted flexure which aerodynamic stresses

**Left: The F-16 that never was – the forward-swept wing demonstrator proposed to DARPA in the mid-1970s.**

tend to set up, but without an unacceptable weight penalty.

DARPA awarded study funds to GD, Grumman and Rockwell International under a project which started in 1976. Several configurations were studied by GD, including one with canards and an aft-mounted wing, but the final SFW/F-16 design was rejected by DARPA in January 1981 in favour of the Grumman 712 – now designated X-29A.

Both the USAF and US Navy are already considering next-generation fighters, and plan to test-fly technology demonstrators based on current aircraft. Fighting Falcon is a natural candidate for these programmes. In 1986 or 1987 the USAF intends to test-fly a flight-technology demonstrator as part of its study effort into next-generation fighters. This could involve a heavily modified F-16 airframe, perhaps mated with a more modern engine such as the P&W PW1130 derivative of the F100.

### STOVL proposal

The most exotic F-16 derivative currently under study is the STOVL (short takeoff/vertical landing) E7 design offered by GD as a solution to the US Navy's specification TS169. This demanding requirement calls for a technology demonstrator capable of hovering for up to four minutes while using only 5 per cent of its fuel load; accelerating from Mach 0·8 to 1·6 at 35,000ft (10,700m) in only 80 seconds; and carrying out a sustained turn rate of 5·5g at 10,000ft (3,000m).

The service wants the aircraft to be built around existing hardware, so GD plans to mate a delta wing with an F-16-derived fuselage, installing a 28,000lb (12,700kg) thrust General Electric F110 (formerly F101 DFE) turbofan engine. To give hovering ability, an ejector system based on a de Havilland Canada design would be used. Air from the engine fan would be collected in a plenum chamber then used either to help provide vertical lift or to boost forward speed during transition and horizontal flight.

In the case of the Rolls-Royce Pegasus engine used in the British Aerospace Harrier, air from the fan is ducted to the forward pair of swivelling nozzles, while core exhaust is ducted to the rear nozzles – the 'four-poster' configuration. In the hover, the E7 would rely on a 'three-poster' scheme having two forward-located thrust sources and a single aft-mounted vectoring nozzle. The forward thrust component would be provided not by vectored nozzles but by the ejector system.

Fan air would be ejected from a series of nozzles arranged in a fore-and-aft line at the root of each wing. Fuselage and wing-mounted doors would direct the fan air downwards. This flow of fan air would draw a further supply of air through a series of louvres in the upper surface of the wing, augmenting the thrust.

In theory, such a scheme could augment fan-air thrust by a factor of up to 1·7, but in practice the gain will be less. The designers of the ill-fated Rockwell XV-12A of the mid-1970s used an augmentation scheme based on ejectors arranged laterally along the wing, but because of unpredicted losses in augmentor efficiency their creation stubbornly refused to hover. As a result of subsequent research into augmentors, GD considers that the technique is now usable. Its great advantage over afterburning 'four-poster' configurations is that it minimizes ground erosion and heating. The hot 'footprint' left by an afterburning Harrier derivative would allow the take-off point to be detected by infra-red sensors long after the aircraft had departed.

During transition the E7 would duct part of the plenum air to an aft-facing tailpipe, while still supplying some thrust via the ejector system. The core exhaust would be vectored and afterburned in the rear nozzle to balance and accelerate the aircraft. The tailpipe incorporates an afterburner, but this would not be used during transition. In horizontal flight the ejector system would be shut down, and all fan air

ducted to the tail-pipe. The rear nozzle and tailpipe afterburners would be used as required.

There are still formidable technical problems to be solved, particularly with the ejector system, but GD plans to spend $2 million during 1984 on refining its design. Tactical radius and air-to-air performance of the E7 would be lower than that of the Fighting Falcon, but GD expects better manoeuvrability in the air-to-ground role.

**Above: This head-on view of the F-16/XL illustrates the excellent shape of the basic F-16 canopy. The pilot has good downward visibility on both sides of the fuselage.**

**Below: Offered as a STOVL technology demonstrator to meet a US Navy requirement, the E7 is the most drastically modified F-16 proposed to date. Powerplant would be a single GE F110 turbofan.**

# Glossary and abbreviations

| | |
|---|---|
| AIM- | US designation for air-to-air missiles |
| AFB | Air Force Base |
| AGM- | US designation for air-to-surface missiles |
| AFTI | Advanced Fighter Technology Integration |
| Algorithm | Mathematical process for achieving a desired result |
| AMRAAM | Advanced Medium-Range Air-to-Air Missile |
| Analogue | Electronic system in which quantities are represented by electrical signals of variable characteristics, i.e. by electrical analogues |
| ANG | Air National Guard |
| ALR- | US designation for a radar-warning receiver |
| APG- | US designation for a nose-mounted fighter radar |
| APQ- | US designation for jamming system |
| Aspect ratio | Ratio of the span of a wing to its chord |
| ASPJ | Advanced Self-Protection Jammer |
| ASRAAM | Advanced Short-Range Air-to-Air Missile |
| Bypass ratio | Ratio of the total airflow through a turbofan engine to that passing through the core section |
| Camber | Curvature of the centreline of a wing aerofoil |
| Category 3 flight test | Operational stage of US certification process – now called Air Force Development, Test and Evaluation |
| CCV | Control-configured vehicle |
| Centre of pressure | Point at which all the lift on the chord of a wing would act if the distributed pressure were to be replaced by a single resultant force |
| c.g. | Centre of gravity |
| Chord | Imaginary line connecting the leading and trailing edge of a wing |
| CRT | Cathode-ray tube (computer/TV-style display screen) |
| DARPA | Defense Advanced Research Projects Agency |
| dB | Decibel (unit of gain or attenuation) |
| Dead-stick | Flight operation carried out with engine(s) shut down or otherwise inoperative |
| Digital | Electronic system in which quantities are as on/off signals coded to represent numbers |
| Drag-at-lift | Drag created under high-lift flight conditions |
| ECM | Electronic countermeasures |
| ECP | Engineering Change Proposal |
| ECP 350 | MSIP modification scheme |
| Envelope | Engineering term for the area defined by a series of limits |
| Esc | see Escadrille and Escuadron |
| Escadrille | Squadron (Belgium) |
| Escuadron | Squadron (Venezuela) |
| Esk, Eskadrille | Squadron (Danish) |
| EW | Electronic warfare |
| FAéB | Force Aérienne Belge, or Belgian Air Force |
| Fail-operative | System element which will allow a system to continue to operate in its active state in the event of a failure |
| Fail-safe | System element which will revert to a safe condition should it fail |
| FBW | Fly-by-wire (term for electrically signalled flight-control systems) |
| FLIR | Forward-looking infra-red |
| g | Unit of acceleration |
| GAO | General Accounting Office (an investigative branch of the US Congress) |
| GD | General Dynamics |
| GE | General Electric |
| GHz | GigaHertz (Hertz × 1,000,000,000) |
| HUD | Head-up display |
| Hz | Hertz (unit of frequency) |
| I&A | Integration and assembly |
| IDFAF | Israel Defence Force – Air Force |
| IIR | Imaging infra-red |
| I/J-band | Radar frequencies from 8 to 12GHz |
| IOC | Initial operating capability |
| IR | infra-red |
| iron bomb | conventional free-falling high-explosive bomb |
| JTIDS | Joint Tactical Information Distribution System |
| KHz | kiloHertz (Hertz × 1,000) |
| KLu | Koninklijke Luchtmacht, or Royal Netherlands Air Force |
| kT | Kiloton |
| Ku-band | Radar frequencies from 12 to 20GHz |
| LANTIRN | Low-Altitude Navigation and Targeting by Infra-Red at Night |
| Mach | Unit equal to the speed of sound |
| MSIP | Multinational Staged Improvement Programme |
| MTU | Maintenance Training Unit |
| MW | Megawatt |
| nav/attack | Navigation and attack (e.g. 'nav/attack system') |
| Nr | Number (Dutch) |
| OCU | Operational Conversion Unit |
| Pacer Loft | Modification programme for European F-16s |
| P&W | Pratt & Whitney |
| Raster scan | Method of building up a TV-style image on a CRT by scanning the image in a series of lines |
| R&D | Research and development |
| RNethAF | Royal Netherlands Air Force |
| RNoAF | Royal Norwegian Air Force |
| RWR | Radar-warning receiver |
| PRF | Pulse repetition frequency |
| Program | Instructions for a computer |
| Programme | Spelling used to designate a programme of research or work |
| Ps | Engineering abbreviation for specific excess power |
| PSP | Programmable signal processor |
| SCAMP | Supersonic Cruise Aircraft Modification Programme |
| sfc | Specific fuel consumption (unit of fuel consumed per unit of thrust per hour) |
| SFW | Swept-forward wing |
| smart bomb | Free-falling bomb with built-in guidance system |
| Software | One or more programs for a computer |
| Synthetic-aperture radar | Technique by which a small radar antenna on a moving vehicle may simulate a larger unit in terms of resolution |
| TAC | Tactical Air Command |
| Taileron | All-moving tailplane able to move differentially as a substitute for traditional aileron control |
| TFG | Tactical Fighter Group |
| TFS | Tactical Fighter Squadron |
| TFTS | Tactical Fighter Training Squadron |
| TFW | Tactical Fighter Wing |
| Trim drag | Component of drag due to the deflection of an elevator or elevon in order to maintain lateral balance of an aircraft |
| TWT | Travelling-wave tube (power source used in many modern radar) |
| USAF | United States Air Force |
| USN | United States Navy |
| Wave drag | Component of drag resulting from the formation of shock waves |
| Wing loading | Weight of an aircraft divided by the wing area |

# Specification

| | YF-16 | F-16A | F-16/79A | F-16XL |
|---|---|---|---|---|
| Length | 48ft 5in/14.75m | 49ft 6in/15.09m | 49ft 6in/15.09m | 54ft 2in/16.51m |
| Wingspan | 31ft 0in/9.45m | 31ft 0in/9.45m | 31ft 0in/9.45m | 34ft 3in/40.92m |
| Height | 16ft 3in/4.95m | 16ft 8in/5.08m | 16ft 8in/5.08m | 17ft 7in/5.36m |
| Weights | | | | |
| Empty | 13,595lb/6,167kg | 15,586lb/7,070kg | 17,041lb/7,730kg | |
| take-off (air-to-air) | 21,600lb/9,798kg | 23,810lb/10,800kg | | |
| Maximum take-off | 27,000lb/12,247kg | 35,400lb/16,057kg | 35,400lb/16,057kg | |
| Wing area | 300sq ft/27.87sq m | 300sq ft/27.87sq m | 300sq ft/27.87sq m | 646sq ft/60.02sq m |
| Wing loading (air-to-air) | | 731lb/sq ft/30.81kg/sq m | | |
| Thrust:weight ratio (air-to-air) | | 1.1:1 | | |
| Maximum speed | Mach 1.95 | >Mach 2 | >Mach 2 | |
| Service ceiling | >50,000ft/15,200m | >50,000ft/15,200m | | |
| Range | | | | |
| Ferry (with ext. tanks) | | >2,100nm/3,890km | | |
| Tactical radius | | >500nm/925km | | c.730nm/1,340km |
| Internal fuel | | 6,972lb/3,162kg | | c.12,700lb/5,760kg |
| No. of hardpoints | | nine | nine | 17 |
| Maximum ordnance load | | 20,450lb/9,280kg | 15,200lb/6,890kg | |

# USAF F-16 units

| Wing | Base | Tail code |
|---|---|---|
| **Tactical Air Command** | | |
| **9th Air Force** | | |
| 56th TTW | Macdill AFB, Florida | MC |
| 363rd TFW | Shaw AFB, South Carolina | SW |
| **12th Air Force** | | |
| 388th TFW | Hill AFB, Utah | HL |
| 474th TFW | Nellis AFB, Nevada | NA, WA |
| **832nd Air Division** | | |
| 58th TTW | Luke AFB, Arizona | LA |
| **US Air Forces in Europe** | | |
| **16th Air Force** | | |
| 401st TFW | Torrejon, Spain | TJ |
| **17th Air Force** | | |
| 50th TFW | Hahn AB, West Germany | HR |
| **Pacific Air Forces** | | |
| **5th Air Force** | | |
| **314th Air Division** | | |
| 8th TFW | Kunsan AB, South Korea | WP |
| **Air National Guard** | | |
| 169th TFG | McEntire ANGB, South Carolina | |

# Picture credits

The publishers wish to thank the following organizations who have supplied photographs for this book:

**Page 4:** both GD. **5:** GD. **6:** top left: Texas Instruments; centre: GD. **7:** both GD. **8:** top left: US Department of Defense; top right and bottom: GD. **9:** top left: GD; top right: USAF; bottom: US Department of Defense; **10:** both GD. **11:** Fokker. **12:** Fokker. **13:** SABCA. **14–15:** both GD. **16:** GD. **17:** both GD. **18:** top: GD; bottom: Belgian Air Force. **19:** GD. **21:** Belgian Air Force. **22:** US Department of Defense. **23:** centre left: USAF; centre right: GD. **24:** top: USAF; bottom: US Department of Defense. **25:** both Pratt & Whitney. **26:** USAF. **27:** top: Pratt & Whitney; bottom: Marconi Avionics. **28:** USAF. **29:** both Pratt & Whitney. **30:** top: Westinghouse; bottom: Marconi Avionics. **31:** both GD. **33:** top: USAF; bottom: Westinghouse. **34:** both Westinghouse. **35:** top: GD; bottom left and right: Marconi Avionics. **36:** Marconi Avionics. **37:** Top and bottom: US Department of Defense; centre: Westinghouse. **38:** Top: GD; centre left: Lear Siegler; centre right: Netherlands Ministry of Defense. **40:** top: USAF; bottom: GD. **41:** top: GD; centre left: British Aerospace Dynamics; centre right: US Department of Defense; bottom: General Electric. **42:** Hughes Aircraft. **43:** GD. **44:** top left and lower right: GD; top right: Texas Instruments; bottom left: Hughes Aircraft. **45:** top: GD; bottom: Kongsberg Vapenfabrikk. **46:** USAF. **47:** top: GD; bottom: USAF. **48:** both USAF. **49:** all USAF. **50:** upper left and top: Royal Netherlands Air Force; lower left and bottom: Belgian Air Force. **51:** top: GD; bottom: Royal Danish Air Force. **52:** both GD. **53:** both GD. **56:** both GD. **57:** top: USAF; bottom: GD. **58–9:** all GD. **60:** top: Vehicle Systems Development Corp; bottom: GD. **61:** both GD. **62:** GD. **63:** GD

PRINTED IN BELGIUM BY

proost
INTERNATIONAL BOOK PRODUCTION